The Importance of Bal

in Life and Business

John Purnell
The Anglepoise Way

Sir Kenneth Grange \

The Anglepoise is a minor miracle of balance.

Balance is a quality in life that we do not value as we should.

\ Industrial Designer

Introduction \
The Anglepoise Way

This book is an overview of 'The Anglepoise Way', which supports a balanced approach to life in general and many of the topics should be looked at from that viewpoint – 'why and how does this affect what we do at Anglepoise, but also how could it help me personally and in my wider life?'

We're also not saying that everything in this book is absolutely what we do, but it is an aspiration of what we think and what we continually strive to be.

Overall this book is a refinement of more than twenty years of experience and research into great company cultures and fundamental principles, but more importantly how to put these principles into practice in a complimentary and effective way. They form a collection of suggestions and advice of how great individuals, teams and companies deliver excellence, whilst always considering 'how do I make this work for me?', and 'how can I personalise this?' as that is the critical factor to success.

About the Author \
John Purnell

John, Managing Director at Anglepoise, has over 20 years of experience successfully growing award winning businesses, fundamentally focussing on their people first and creating a company culture of purpose, authenticity and excellence.

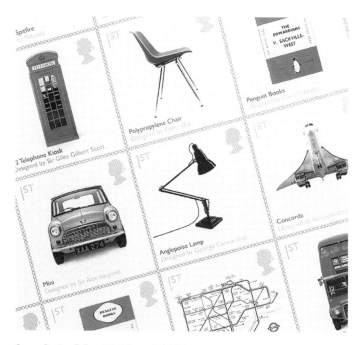

About Anglepoise \

A Timeless British Brand

In 1932, when vehicle suspension engineer George Carwardine invented a spring, crank and lever mechanism that could be positioned with the lightest of touch yet would maintain its position once released, a blueprint for the first Anglepoise task lamp was born. The Anglepoise lamp has subsequently achieved iconic status and its engaging, anthropomorphic form is recognised and admired all around the world.

Over the years, the Anglepoise lamp has been developed under the careful watch of the founding Terry family, without ever losing sight of its primary function, and unique, characterful form.

From the creation of the Original 1227™ lamp, to the development of extended collections by esteemed industrial product designer Sir Kenneth Grange, to recent collaborations with renowned designers Paul Smith and Margaret Howell, incomparable British design remains at the heart of this progressive British brand. Today, Anglepoise lamps can be found in homes and offices, restaurants, bars and hotels in more than 50 countries.

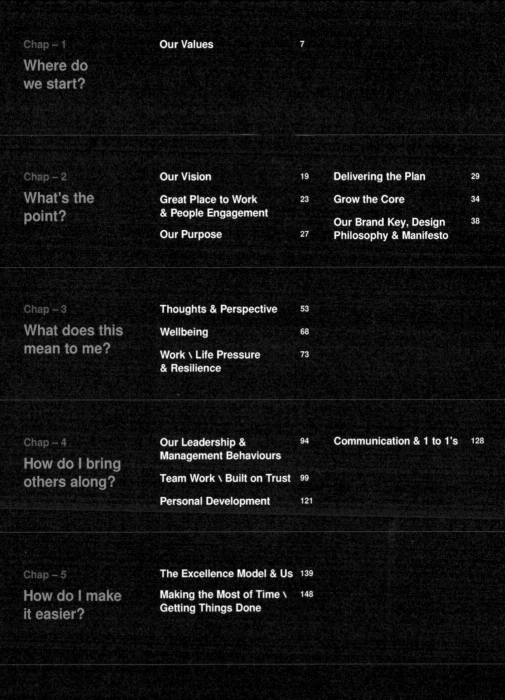

1

Values & Guiding Principles

1–8

Do you wish
to rise? Begin
by descending.
You plan a tower
that will pierce the
clouds? Lay first
the foundation
of humility.

From little acorns do mighty oaks grow.

Always Build on
Solid Foundations

As with all things we should start at the beginning and whether it's a person, plant, business or building, your foundations are what make you strong. For a plant it would be the location, environment and nourishment from the soil; for a building it would be the depth, material and quality of the foundations; and for us it is our core values (both business and personal) that establish the solidity and certainty from what everything is then built upon.

But what are your 'values' (could also be considered as your 'guiding principles')? Well, they're what make you 'you', they're the things that are inherent and fundamental about us as individuals, and they're the core of the culture of Anglepoise the business.

Values are what help us to make decisions and decide on what is the right thing to do. Values are the strong foundations that we must build from and then act upon in everything we do. They must never be the poster on the office wall gathering dust, but what we live and breathe, what our hearts pound for and define us, and how we see the world.

When you think about your personal values, consider what is critical to you? What instincts help you to make the right decisions and do the right thing? How do you morally live your life, and bring up your children or guide the next generation – all of these actions will be based upon your personal values, and we believe as a business they should act as the bedrock of all that we do.

That is why our values are integrated into everything we do, from recruitment to personal development; from product development to marketing and the overall culture (or DNA) of Anglepoise is defined by them.

The rest of this book will cover what each of these values means to us both at Anglepoise and personally, also providing guidance and examples of these principles in practice.

Our Values

PURPOSE

In everything we do understand why

AUTHENTICITY

Keep it real whilst respecting others

LEADERSHIP

We are all leaders playing to our strengths

Continuous improvement along the journey

Doing the right thing now for the future

9

Purpose, Vision & Goals

9 — 44

It's not enough
to have lived.

We should be
determined to live
for something.

John F. Kennedy \

Efforts and courage are not enough without purpose and direction.

\ 35th U.S. President

In Everything We Do
Understand Why

 Purpose

Everything starts with understanding why? What's the point? Why does whatever we're considering doing, actually need doing? What's the purpose or outcome, and why is that necessary? Does it fit into our overall plan (our strategy)? and so on.

But we need to always understand the **fundamental** why, and not the potentially 'superficial' why.

We can use 5 why analysis (or why / why) techniques to achieve this – where you continue asking yourself the why question for each answer until you can go no further and you should have the fundamental why and purpose, and only then you can decide if it's worth doing.

Another good way of looking at if you've found the fundamental why is ask yourself 'what if I now don't do this at all, what difference would it make in a month or even a year'. Or imagine yourself in a year from now – did it makes any difference?, if the answer is very little or not at all, then don't do it.

Once you've determined the fundamental why and agreed it meets the overall plan, only then can you effectively implement it using the rest of our values and guidance in this book.

A great tool that we use to help remind us that we should always start with the end in mind and understand the fundamental why and purpose is RADAR from the EFQM. This will be covered in more detail (in Chap – 5), but is very relevant to helping us understand everything starts with purpose, before actually doing anything.

Using the RADAR process below start with Step 1
before any other action is taken to ensure it's worth
doing and meets the overall plan (or strategy).

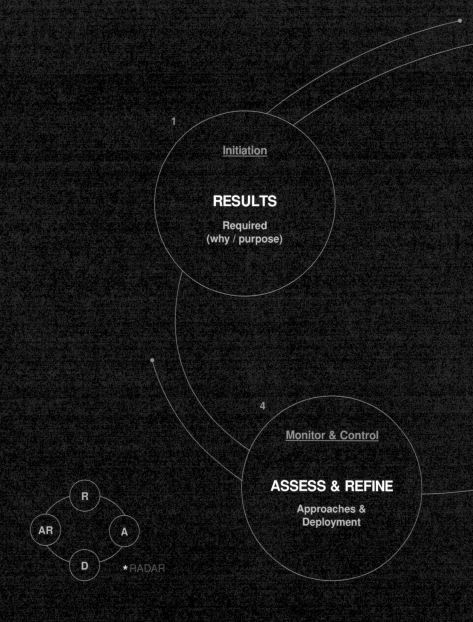

1

Initiation

RESULTS

Required
(why / purpose)

4

Monitor & Control

ASSESS & REFINE

Approaches &
Deployment

R

AR   A

D   *RADAR

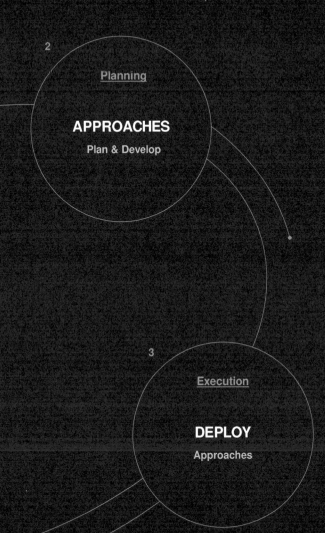

2

<u>Planning</u>

APPROACHES

Plan & Develop

3

<u>Execution</u>

DEPLOY

Approaches

But, it's still all about the journey...

We're also great believers that it's all about the journey, not the destination.

So what do we mean by this? Well the destination should be the overall outcome you're striving for once you've agreed that the fundamental why meets the plan and is worth doing. This is then what you're aiming for and is obviously still important, particularly for teams or a company so that everyone is pulling is the same direction. But far more important is enjoying the journey to get there, the day to day activities and successes that should be celebrated, and we should be as contented and in the moment as much as possible, playing to our strengths and savouring all that we enjoy and do.

So, whilst we should always **start with the end in mind** – knowing our destination and guiding light – we should also strive to enjoy each step of the journey that we take, both personally and in our teams, with perspective, grace and humility.

Personal **belief** in the purpose or goal is also very important – not 'I **think** we can do this'... but 'I **know** we can do this... it's the right thing to do, and I'm going to make it happen'. It's important that we're all emotionally engaged and believe in the cause and outcome, hence why we focus so much as a business on our 'people engagement'.

Another key theme in this book and 'The Anglepoise Way' is always remembering that you have a choice – **life is all about choice** – no one forces you to go to work, to do the job that you do, therefore choose to be engaged, to give your best for the greater good, both for the company and your own personal development and success.

If you're **choosing** what you want to do, you shouldn't (only perhaps incredibly rarely) ever need to say 'I **have** to do... anything' (except eat, drink and sleep of course), you should be always thinking and saying 'I **want** to do... something' – you should be **choosing** to do all that you do, always, and if that isn't the case then choose to do something else, or even be somewhere else.

And finally we should always be looking for **insights not just information** – we're not preparing for a quiz, we're trying to understand or confirm that what we're currently doing is right or change our course of action, and if so, to what.

Apply the **'That's interesting... but so what?'** test to all that you're choosing to do to confirm that it is indeed the right thing to do for the right reasons.

So, bearing all of this in mind what's the compelling or **fundamental why** and purpose for Anglepoise?

Our Vision

Our Vision should always be our guiding light, the aspiration of what we are always striving to achieve.

It's deliberately in order of importance and so we start with 'Great Place to Work' effectively meaning we put our people first in all of our decision making, based on our values, and always aiming for Anglepoise to be the best workplace culture possible, taking into account everyone's personal characteristics, needs and requirements.

Great Place to Work

2 **Customers Delighted**

3 **Love the Products**

4 **Proud of Anglepoise**

5 **Culture of Excellence**

Great Place to Work

My Company

I'm proud to work here, it's fun, I'm engaged and making a difference.

Leadership

If the leadership's good, so's the management. I believe in our goals and values.

My Manager

I get on really well with my manager, they support and develop me.

Fair Deal

The company values me, my pay and benefits are good.

My Team

I have friends and I'm supported, there's a real team spirit.

Personal Growth

My skills are fully used. I'm challenged, and can progress.

Wellbeing

I have appropriate pressure, and my work and home life is perfectly balanced.

Giving Back

It's not just about the company, it's also the wider community.

Great Place to Work
& People Engagement

Our overall approach to this is based around the 'Great Place to Work' framework (adapted from 'Best Companies' and principles from 'Investors in People') which we've now used for many years.

Some time ago we started the ongoing process of trying to build a great place to work around the framework above, creating many outstanding approaches, policies and procedures in all areas (particularly around flexibility and work / life balance), but most importantly ensuring everyone was trained in them and they became what we 'live and breathe' each day, whilst still always looking for improvements.

It's also very important to ensure everyone has a clear understanding what we mean by certain key approaches and phrases we use in the business and therefore having broad definitions of each can help to provide clarity of meaning and purpose.

Our Definition of
A Great Place to Work

Our goal to become a Great Place to Work means:

We are characterised by our creativity, pride, flexibility and professionalism.

We have workplaces where people choose to work, give freely of their energies and feel a sense of personal achievement, satisfaction, individual purpose and security.

We have a synergy between personal missions and work challenges, and organisational achievement.

A critical element to a great place to work is around our people engagement, always looking at maximising how we can engage everyone in the business and beyond.

Engagement being a strong positive emotional connection from everyone to each other and the business, a belief in each other and the purpose of Anglepoise, and always acting for the greater good of both.

Our Definition of
People Engagement

People Engagement at Anglepoise means:

Creating an environment where everyone is motivated to want to connect with their work and really care about doing a great job.

Creating opportunities for everyone to connect with their colleagues, managers and wider organisation.

It is a concept that places flexibility, change and continuous improvement at the heart of what it means to work at Anglepoise.

We believe that if we can achieve a great place to work and high levels of people engagement then everything else follows – delighted customers who are advocates, through to an ongoing sustainable successful business.

Delighting customers (both internal and external) must be the desired goal as simply meeting their needs is not enough. We have a separate 'Delight the Customer' strategy and action team focussed on delivering just this, via our overarching business framework the excellence model.

Moving on to **Love the Products** and **Proud of Anglepoise**, both thoughtfully using very emotive words because these should always be fundamental to what we do. In all products we ever design and create, they must be able to be loved, not just liked. Our products should be with our customers for their life's journey and love is a crucial part of that.

We should also be true to our **values** in all that we do, and every action we take (again both internal and external) should embody something we will be proud of. **Pride**, and we mean **stand up hand on heart**, should be what we're always aiming for, such that everyone who works for us or with us are genuinely proud to do so.

Lastly **Culture of Excellence**, at its most simple, we should always be looking to improve what we do; question everything and find better ways – evolution not revolution, incremental continuous improvement (more detail in Chap – 5).

Our Purpose

To have a 'great place to work' that enables everyone to play to their strengths; empowering us all to do the right thing.

We aim to delight our customers and partners.

Through care and attention to detail we design timeless products that are a pleasure to use and are loved.

To develop an organisation, brand and products that people feel proud to be a part of.

We will work together to continuously improve on our journey to excellence.

We've decided to take the approach that our purpose should just add more detail to our vision, so there's a common thread that makes sense and also becomes a common language and understanding within our culture. Our purpose can also be considered as the 'why we're here'.

So, we've defined our '**why** and **purpose**' at different levels, but what about **how** and **what** we will do to actually achieve this.

An overused word in business is 'Strategy', too often a 'management' term used to make people sound more impressive and self-important, whilst also sadly distancing different parts of the workplace teams by unnecessary hierarchical language.

Quite simply 'Strategy' is a plan of action designed to achieve long-term or overall goals, so basically just our long-term plan, and the main approach we take to this is via our Mission (effectively key goals for the coming year), and our Balanced Scorecard.

Delivering the Plan
& Mission

Our '**What** and **How**' – via the Balanced Scorecard
approach (originally developed by Kaplan and Norton),
closely integrates with the balanced results requirements
of the excellence model (from the EFQM) and ensures that
we're measuring the delivery of our overall plan in a very
balanced way, both in terms of short and long term goals,
and across all key areas of the business – Financial,
Business Processes, Customers (external and internal),
and Learning and Growth.

We use this on a monthly basis at our Senior Leadership
team meetings to quickly assess key areas of focus in need
of prioritisation and support, whilst celebrating our successes
where appropriate. The simple traffic light coded measures
make this simple at a glance, and this information is then
also shared company-wide every month and at our quarterly
Compass meetings (where the senior leadership team share
updates across all areas of the business in a honest and frank
manner, also focussing on key activities going forwards).

On the following page is a high-level example of our
Balanced Scorecard with the details removed to give you
a flavour of what's important to us. It's also worth noting
that behind all of these areas is a substantial amount of
evidence and measurement, and in many cases departmental
KPI's (Key Performance Indicators), with individual monthly
and quarterly targets from each team members Personal
Development Reviews (set annually and updated monthly
where appropriate via 1 to 1 meetings), so that as far as
practical everyone has 'line of sight' from what they do day
to day and the overall impact to the wider success of the
business.

Our Balanced Scorecard

Financial

Turnover Growth	
Gross Profit Margin	%
Min Monthly Cash	%
Non-UK Sales	%
UK Contract Sales	%
	%

1

Processes

Financial Delivery	%
Product Development	%
Delivery of Sales	%
Health & Safety	%
Supplier Scorecards	%
Brand & Marketing	%

2

Vision & Strategy

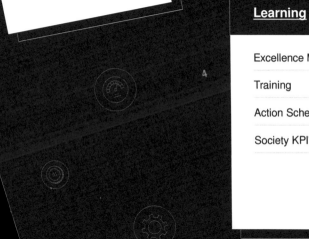

<u>Learning</u>

Excellence Model	%
Training	%
Action Scheme	%
Society KPI's	%

Our Mission

Ensure Anglepoise is a Great Place to Work by achieving people engagement survey levels in excess of x / x

By delighting our customers, our Net Promoter Score (NPS) will exceed x %

Our group revenues will be at least £ x with a gross margin > x %

Our international sales will exceed x % of revenue (U.S. x %) and UK Contracts x %

On our journey to excellence our annual assessment will exceed x points.

Our Mission statement flows through from our Vision and Purpose and captures our annual high level / priority targets to achieve our overall plan (strategy). More important are the breakdown of detailed plans and activities behind each of these, many of which are captured and tracked on the **Balanced Scorecard**.

Grow the Core

Another key part to our overall growth plan is to '**Grow the Core**', as you can see focussed at the centre of our **Balanced Scorecard**.

This is a process based around the excellent book by David Taylor (from Brand Gym), where we've used and adapted many of the approaches to clarify and define exactly what our 'Core' is and determine the action plans to successfully grow the business in the medium and long term.

A key part of the Grow the Core approach is through detailed external and internal research and evidence gathering, you can then discover an array of insights that help you determine and **understand exactly what your 'Core' is** – focussing primarily on your: **Source of Margin** and **Source of Authority**.

Our **'Source of Margin'** is at its simplest understanding where we deliver the most of our margin from, by way of product type, customers, regions, etc. and the relative size of that margin and if it's growing. This is then encouraging you to focus on selling more of the stuff you already sell, as opposed to new products / services for the sake of it.

Our **'Source of Authority'** is determining and understanding what we're known for, and what we're famous for. What do we have authority and authenticity for and why?

Once the **'Core'** is fully understood and agreed (after a substantial amount of research and work), we can then use the other approaches in the book to determine our priorities and plan of action. Two key considerations follow.

Key Core
Growth Drivers

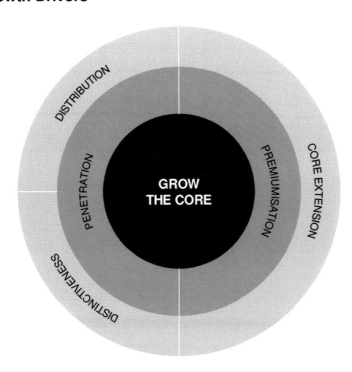

Once you know your 'Core' this is a great tool to focus your growth plans on increasing customer and market penetration (e.g. through increased global distribution, and distinctiveness of your product offering), and through 'premiumisation' of your product and service offering, looking to extend your core range, but always referencing your source of margin and authority.

Core Ideas
The Brand and Business Building Potential

Another key tool to help select which themes and ideas should be turned into action is shown below. Ideally 80%–90% of all growth projects and actions should have high business and brand vision build (Cash Builders and Hero's), with only a small focus on pure Brand Image building, and obviously none that would be a drain.

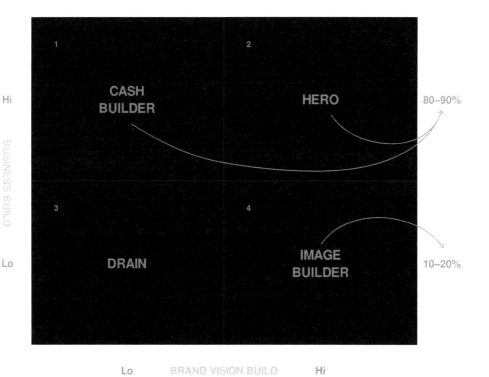

Our Brand Key, Design Philosophy & Manifesto

The final part of our fundamental why and what we're here for can be best described by the work from our close partnership with Sir John Hegarty and his team from The Garage Soho, where we've produced the following for our brand key, design philosophy and brand manifesto. This is more specifically around our brand and product design aspirations but also encapsulates who we are:

Brand Vision
Create an Anglepoise Legacy for the next generation.

Brand Discriminator
Only Anglepoise is for life.

Brand Key
Roots, Our Customers, Functional & Emotional Benefit, Human & Product Truth
(see more on page 39).

Brand Personality
As a product we are a British icon – definitive but slightly eccentric. Familiar and dependable therefore, but ever evolving, ever surprising, human and even playful.

As a company we want to be 'open' to our customers and consumers. We feel we are in a relationship with them over time, not just for a transaction. We want them to feel part of us, not just be customers.

\ Roots

Bringing an engineering 'problem solving' point of view to life for over 80 years and 5 generations of the Terry family.

All with the common goal of building a company and products that we can truly value, love and be proud of… and become a legacy to pass onto next generations.

\ Emotional Benefit

Like a friend – reassuringly always 'there' for me. My Anglepoise helps me and supports me to:

\ Illuminate my life
\ Focus
\ Switch on and switch off
\ Anchors me in the world

And so, like a long-term friend it makes me smile the smile of recognition and appreciation.

\ Human Truth

The world is suffering from a throw away culture – too much stuff, too many trends, built for disposability and not to last.

Yet what we value most in our lives are the constants – the things that become part of our lives and treasured possessions, not just mere 'things'.

There is a growing movement to recognise this. We can lead that movement.

\ Our Customers

Anglepoise is loved by a small group of design lovers who see it as an icon. We need to share that love to a wider, younger, next generation of 'do-ers' and become their first task light of choice.

We will become their 'light for life' – from their first space, to first house, to family home, to passing onto their own children.

\ Functional Benefit

Built to last a lifetime – Anglepoise grows and evolves as the people it serves do, therefore it will never become outdated. Because my Anglepoise is built:

\ To last (guaranteed for life)
\ To be a joy to touch (tactile materials)
\ To be responsive (fingertip control and balance)
\ To be useful for the task at hand and versatile in how I use it

And therefore, to constantly evolve and surprise me

\ Product Truth

The Long View – The Anglepoise way, a design philosophy that rejects disposability.

Our Design Philosophy \
The Long View

We believe in The Long View. In creating a culture,
a relationship with our customers and our users, and
of course products, that last beyond the moment.

We are anti-disposability.

Too much stuff is made today and gone tomorrow,
made to be thrown away. We feel and think that can
only be damaging, both for our planet and our souls.

Creating a world that is throwaway, to our minds, fosters
a throwaway mind set. Surrounding ourselves with too
many things can only clutter our heads.

Worrying about the latest and newest can only leave you
– well, worried!

Surely the best things in life are the things that are built
to last – that are a constant companion, that stay with us,
that become almost part of us.

In Everything we do we First Understand Why

Our products look like they do because they solve a human problem, serving a purpose, fit for the task in hand.

Principle – 1

It's Better to do One Thing Exceptionally Well

Focus brings learnings, experience and knowledge.

Principle – 2

Durability is a Joy

We build using methods and materials that will last. Our products are guaranteed for life because we feel things should last a lifetime, and even beyond.

Principle – 3

Responsive Products that Encourage Interaction

We choose materials and details that invite the human touch, that are a pleasure to use. We design for elegance, proportion, balance and fingertip responsiveness.

Principle – 4

We Design to Create a Smile

The objects that become possessions and a treasured possession in our lives are the ones that somehow, we become attached to – that make us smile.

We Pursue Openness

We want everyone we interact with to feel part of us. We pursue feedback to learn, adapt and always improve everything we do. We foster collaborations with like-minded partners, for the greater good.

Authenticity with Delight

We will remain true to our iconic heritage guided by the original principles and ideas that created the Anglepoise. But we will aim to constantly surprise and delight within that authentic vision. After all we do want to make people smile when using our products.

Loved Beyond a Lifetime

In short, we are led by the overriding principle of taking The Long View and of growing a company and creating products that are built to last. Even to be loved, for a lifetime and beyond.

Our Brand Manifesto

What do you see when you switch on an Anglepoise?

A pool of light,

or a lamp illuminating brilliance?

The book you're reading,

the music you're playing,

the design you're creating,

or even the cake you're baking.

A design that functions not flirts.

A spring-loaded tool…

that adopts whatever position you command.

A symbol of permanence in a world of obsolescence.

That switches on your imagination,

turning darkness into light.

With a reassuring click.

On and off.

We're not just a lamp,

we're an Anglepoise...

made for life.

A life we guarantee.

ANGLEPOISE®

Abandon Darkness.

Authenticity

45 – 86

Brene Brown \

Authenticity is a collection of choices that we make every day. It's about the choice to show up and be real. The choice to be honest. The choice to let our true selves be seen.

\ Research Professor

Authenticity is more than speaking. Authenticity is also about doing. Every decision we make says something about who we are.

\\ Author & Motivational Speaker

Keep It Real Whilst Respecting Others

 Authenticity

'Know yourself, be yourself' – it may sound obvious but how well do we really understand who we are and want to be, rather than what we think others want us to be, or expect us to be.

At Anglepoise we try to help everyone to better understand themselves and embrace that, and then we can better **respect** each other and all of our differences.

We start with a strong focus on your personal **talents** and **strengths** using the significant research and subsequent tools created by Marcus Buckingham and the Gallup organisation (now by Don Clifton and Tom Rath in 'Strengths Finder 2').

This global research strongly shows that by focussing on our natural instinctive talents and over time turning them into strengths, will we then consistently perform at our best, and most importantly enjoy every minute doing it.

When we are doing something which is an instinctive strength we are typically 'in the zone' and time just flies by because it's 'just what we're great at'. We almost don't know why we're doing our best work, just that it feels so easy because we're in that natural state of flow where everything works.

Using the online 'strengths finder' assessment you're given your top 5 strengths (amongst 34) and a variety of examples of what that means to many different people in a variety of roles. These strengths are complimentary in that they each affect your other top strengths to help you (and your colleagues) to better understand how you can do your best work every day.

All of our personal development approaches focus on how we can maximise our strengths (see Chap – 4 for more detail) and whilst you can't ignore your areas of development, that should be just 'damage limitation' only, or even better, find someone else in the team who has strength in that area and reassign the work accordingly.

Clearly our workplace isn't a utopia where everyone loves every second of every day and is playing to their strengths and are always 'in the zone', but that's certainly our aspiration, because why wouldn't it be – everyone enjoying what they do and being great at it – work isn't meant to be hard, it should be interesting, fun, engaging and providing a sense of fulfilment.

By understanding our strengths and those of our team mates we can also better understand how we all work best together – the right activities, done by the right people at the best time, in a way that also suits them (also hence our approach to different forms of flexible working).

Honesty

'Be truthful and sincere, whilst respecting others' – It hopefully goes without saying that we should all be honest both with ourselves and others, as whilst that's obviously 'the right thing to do' it also achieves betters outcomes, with greater clarity, more efficiency, consistency and success.

A key part to honesty and trust is doing what you say – many of us have heard of the **SAY** / **DO** gap – where ideally there should never be a gap, and we all **DO** what we **SAY** (or update people if there is some good reason why we can no longer do what we've said).

When there is any gap between what we say and what we do then there can be mistrust and a loss of belief, both in the individual and the cause or purpose. So, being authentic, only say what you actually believe and are choosing to do.

Perhaps a good example of a common and deliberate **SAY** / **DO** gap (which we should always avoid) is a statement you may hear in sales and customer support in that you should 'under promise and over deliver', but if you're being authentic and honest then even with the best of intentions that statement is at best misleading and at worst, borderline lying.

Again, being authentic, any communication, whether that's to customers (e.g. you should receive the product by Friday, knowing that they'll probably get in on Tuesday), or colleagues at work (e.g. I think this will take me 3 days, but I'll say a week and then look good when I deliver early), are both examples of deliberate **SAY** / **DO** gaps and must be avoided – **think** about what you can realistically and pragmatically do, **SAY** that, and then **DO** it (this also strongly links to Chap – 4 – Leadership and trust).

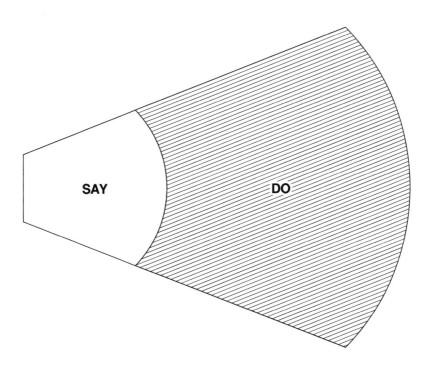

Thoughts & Perspective

Thoughts & Thinking

Thoughts are just that – thinking that goes on in your head, tens of thousands of times a day.

I've always loved Einstein's quote – **'Reality is just an illusion, all be it a very persistent one'** – our 'reality' is determined by our thoughts, and our thoughts determine how we see the world, how we feel, and then how we act.

But even after generations of research by scientists, psychologists, philosophers, etc. there is still no firm consensus of defining what thought actually is.

There is a huge amount of research and information available about our thinking and how it can impact our lives very substantially, for better or worse, but that certainly is not the point of this chapter of the book (as that would be many books in itself), however understanding some of the key principles that we believe in can help us to better understand ourselves and therefore be more authentic.

So, for practical purposes we can broadly consider 'Thought' to be reactions within the brain, due to some stimulation or another and based on a multitude of factors, both in your past but more importantly in the moment (for instance: surroundings; health; climate; noise; smells; perspective; history; upbringing; education; etc.).

Your perceived significance of these thoughts can vary hugely depending on the above circumstances and your rational or irrational perspective of them in the moment.

Fundamentally though these are only thoughts, not facts, and in the majority of cases particularly if you're considering your thoughts irrationally and without perspective, likely to be misguided and overstated, and they're further likely to be having an unnecessary negative impact on you and your subsequent feelings and actions.

Perhaps one way to help us to understand and appreciate the actual insignificance of negative or difficult thoughts (or even all thoughts) can possibly be achieved by considering the amount of thoughts we have in a typical day – if you were to have a new thought every second (or even a thought on a thought) and say that you're awake 17 hours a day, then 17 hours x 60 minutes x 60 seconds would = 61,200 thoughts every day!

Even if you feel you only have a thought every 2 seconds that's still more than 30,000 thoughts a day (not including any thoughts during your sleep). ⇁

Therefore, is it really surprising that you may have 100+ bad, negative or worrying thoughts a day in the midst of all that. But that's less than 0.2% a day, and in the overall % scheme of your thoughts it's negligible or even totally irrelevant.

Again, we need to remember they're only thoughts…imagine if you said out loud every thought that came into your head… clearly thoughts are not statements of fact (and they still don't become facts just because you say them!).

Imagine a **'Thoughtometer'** (like below), e.g. 60,000 thoughts in a day and 100 of them are negative or worrying thoughts… see how insignificant they are compared to everything else – see them for what they are – just thoughts, not facts – let the thoughts pass and another will come along, like clouds in the sky, or waves upon the beach…

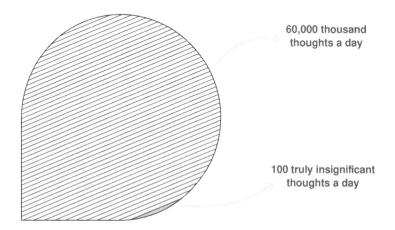

60,000 thousand
thoughts a day

100 truly insignificant
thoughts a day

If we can accept that all of our thoughts are not facts, just fleeting reactions in our heads, then we can better control the impact on our feeling and actions.

A significant amount of research and best practice strongly ties your Thoughts → Feelings → Actions as below, but it typically starts with your thoughts:

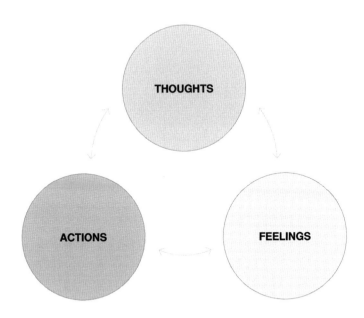

Using mindfulness (which almost everyone at Anglepoise has had training for) and other techniques we can better understand and accept our thoughts without letting them always control our feelings and actions. Particularly negative thoughts which can lead to poor feelings and outcomes which just make the situation worse and often could be avoided.

Another very useful approach to remember is that you can only ever '**control the controllables**'. I believe this approach originates and is very popular with athletes and sports teams, and is also closely linked to mindfulness, in that when you have perspective and are in the moment anything outside of your control and influence (the uncontrollables) should be let go of, and only focus your time, effort and energy on the things that you can actually do something about. You are then choosing to take action on something that you can actually change and make a difference.

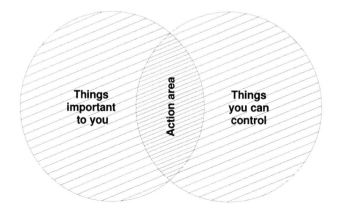

Perspective

What actually is 'Perspective' and why is it important?
Here are some definitions: 'a particular attitude towards or
way of regarding something'; 'a point of view'; 'comparing,
seeing from afar'; 'ideally looking at something from a
balanced, non-biased view-point'.

Consider the image below...

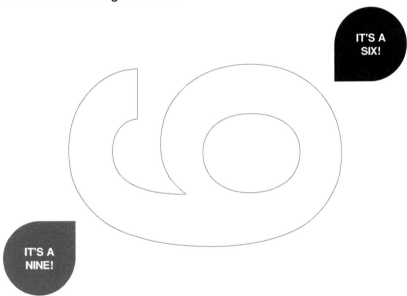

**Just because you're right, does not mean, I am wrong.
You just haven't seen life from my side.**

I'm sure you've heard the suggestion when you perhaps don't have a balanced perspective to '**Put yourself in someone else's shoes**', this is apparently based on the old Native Indian saying of 'Walking in another person's shoes / moccasins' – and whilst it can be useful to take a step back and reconsider your view, you have to think more deeply about how credible this approach is.

> **You can try and see it from the other persons perspective but you will have you own view of the world based on your values, beliefs, experience, filters and perhaps personal psychological 'baggage' – to see it exactly from their perspective you would literally need to be them – with all their history, upbringing, education, experience etc.**

An example from an Emotional Intelligent training course I did many years ago asked the question 'Would you have invaded Iraq if you were George Bush?' (feel free to update this to a similarly weighty question from today)... a variety of opinions ensued from everyone on the course about what they may have done differently if they were George Bush faced with that decision, but ultimately it's nonsense, if **you were actually** George Bush, 100% George Bush, then you would have made **exactly** the same decision and invaded Iraq because that's precisely what he did, and so to truly put yourself in someone else's shoes, would to become fully them and take exactly the same actions – surely impossible for any of us.

However taking this approach at the right level and expectation can help you to detach yourself from your current thinking and realise that what you 'think' is important, may not actually be, or at least you now appreciate the other viewpoint and respect that, even if you still disagree.

Perspective also gives us relevancy and understanding of how important things actually are, and to different people, and most importantly 'why' it's relevant and important. Often when you seek advice from someone you respect and trust, you seek perspective.

To consistently gain perspective in life as a daily habit and routine, different things work for different people, but here (next page) are some interesting examples of what works for me and others that I've met over the years.

Seeing the Bigger Picture

Consider a **glass elevator** or **helicopter view** – imagine flying upwards in a helicopter with great views, or like in 'Charlie and the Great Glass Elevator' (by Roald Dahl), you're moving up through the floors in the glass elevator and as you go up you can see more widely but also you gain perspective as you see things in relation to others things, plus you also see that things aren't as 'BIG' as you thought they were, things start to feel less important than when you were down on the ground floor and your thoughts felt more significant and urgent (perhaps the 'monsters' felt more real)… suddenly they look pretty small and trivial. This is similar to the saying, '**Don't make a mountain out of a mole hill**'.

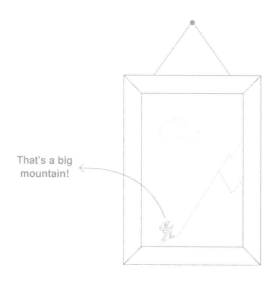

That's a big mountain!

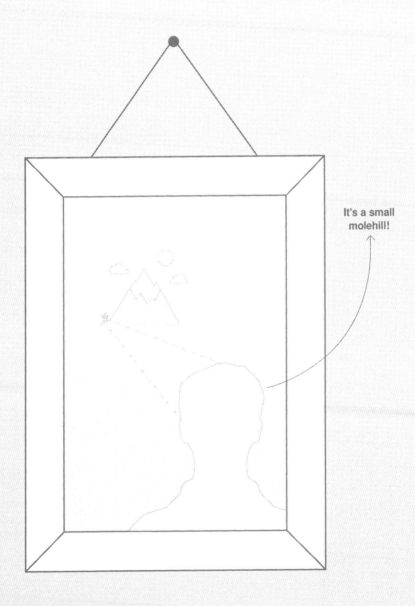

Storm in a Teacup

Another common saying is that something is just a **'Storm in a teacup'**, and that 'something' seems super important at the time and all hells broken lose about a particular problem (this seems to often happen in politics where one party is claiming the other has done something absolutely terrible and they all should resign and fall on their swords), and for me what this is getting at is that if you're in the teacup in the centre of the storm then things really do appear awful and terrible and the end of the world is nigh... but if you're on the edge of the teacup looking down then you can see the storm and how it might appear bad for those stuck in it, but you can also see that in the scheme of things, it's not that big a deal and will 'blow over'.

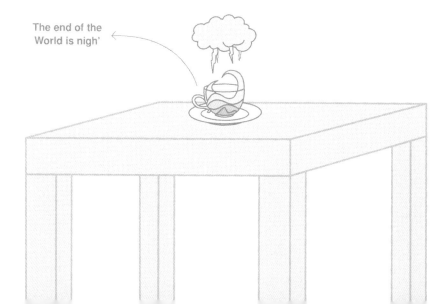

The end of the World is nigh'

Consider then if you were in the corner of the room and can see the cup but not the storm inside then you will have a different less consequential perspective, but imagine that you're not in the room, or even the building, you're in another city, then you can't see the storm, or the tea cup, or any of the potential implications....to that persons perspective it's utterly irrelevant and has no consequence.

This is often where seeking advice from an independent or disconnected person (from the situation) can provide that helpful perspective.

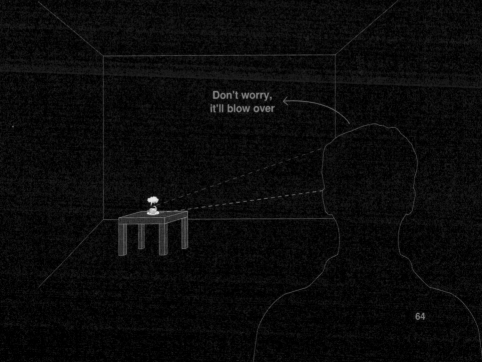

Empty Cinema Theory

Imagine you're sat in an empty cinema / theatre looking up at the screen, but this time rather than your favourite film or show, it's your own thoughts playing in front of you... could you feel a greater sense of detachment from them and perspective, seeing them for what they are – just thoughts, not facts, that can change at any given moment.

Hmm, it's not that
scary from here

Assignment of Meaning

Be conscious of assigning **'meaning'** or **'labels'** to things and thoughts. Compare when you're at your most happy or content and how you react to annoying things or even people… take a bad driver for instance, when you're happy and content – you just let it go, but if you're unhappy, you may get angry with the poor driver and even do something rash yourself like pressing your horn or driving unsafely close to them etc.

If you can at any moment react well to something and 'take it in your stride', then you can do the same at any other moment, it's only your perspective and assignment of meaning that varies due to what you're thinking.

Playing Devil's Advocate

You could also take the approach of acting as **Devil's advocate** – a deliberately provocative view to challenge your thinking even if you totally disagree.

This can be very useful as sometimes we inadvertently (or even deliberately) find ourselves with very similar people who naturally agree with us. This is commonly referred to as living in an **Echo Chamber**, surrounding ourselves at work and home (especially online with social media like Facebook) with similar people, with similar views, effectively therefore not providing any perspective or other point of view.

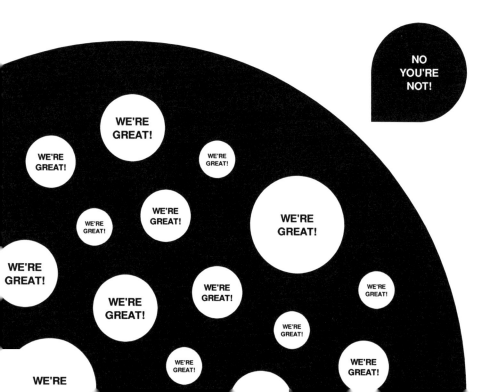

Finally, on perspective I've personally always been a strong advocate of **'Care... but don't care'**. What I mean by that is, when appropriate, remind yourself of the **ultimate perspective.** If you're worrying about meeting some deadline at work, or solving a customer's problem, then yes, really care and do everything you can to achieve that, but when it ultimately comes down to it, there are more important things in life, the things we **fundamentally** personally care about and are core to our very existence.

Wellbeing

Amongst other things, being authentic is about knowing ourselves, seeing our thoughts for what they are and having perspective.

Other important themes to help us be our authentic selves are closely tied into our wellbeing, which is hugely affected by our work / life pressure and our resilience to that, but what actually is wellbeing?

Wellbeing Definitions

From our Great Place
to Work framework
(in Chap – 2):

**I have appropriate pressure,
and my work and home life
is perfectly balanced.**

The World Health
Organization (WHO, 1997)
defines quality of life
(albeit a little wordy) as:

**An individual's perception
of their position in life in
the context of the culture
and value systems in which
they live and in relation to
their goals, expectations,
standards and concerns.
It is a broad ranging concept
affected in a complex way by
the person's physical health,
psychological state, personal
beliefs, social relationships
and their relationship to
salient features of their
environment.**

Shah and Marks consider
wellbeing to be:

**Wellbeing is more than
just happiness. As well as
feeling satisfied and happy,
wellbeing means developing
as a person, being fulfilled,
and making a contribution
to the community.**

It can also be looked at as **balance** or **equilibrium** – each time you meet a **challenge**, the needs (i.e. psychological, social, or physical) of the challenge and resources you have available comes into a state of **imbalance**, as you are forced to adapt your resources to meet the particular challenge.

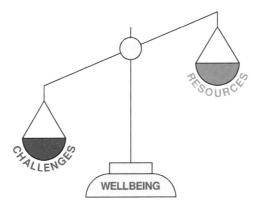

Overall there are many approaches we take at Anglepoise that aim to address wellbeing from many sides (some examples listed below), but perhaps the most important foundation of this is our commitment to **'Time to Change'** and **ending mental health discrimination**, both professionally in the workplace and personally in our lives.

At is most simple this is about enabling everyone to talk about their mental health like they would their physical health, without any discrimination or concern, so that we can all help find the right support and make changes to suit our personal needs.

Our 'Time to Change' Pledges and Ongoing Actions for Wellbeing

Commitment and leadership from the Board / Senior Leadership Team.

Quarterly update at every Compass (company-wide) meeting and sharing newsletters, guidance, films, case studies, promotional materials.

Sharing personal experiences at all levels.

Use of 'Wellness Actions Plans' where appropriate.

Mindfulness training for anyone who is interested, and other stress reduction techniques.

Wellbeing and People Engagement surveys (and more importantly, actions).

Stress at Work training and refreshers.

'Tea and talk' quarterly meetings (voluntary).

Mental health awareness training for all line managers.

Free 'Employee Assistance Program' (EAP).

Quarterly review of progress and appropriateness at H, S & E team meetings

Flexible Working Hours scheme & Homeworking Policy.

Compassionate leave Policy.

Voluntary Social Team with own annual budget for company-wide activities.

Paid charity / community workday.

'Holiday handover process' to encourage proper disconnect when on holiday.

Incentives like cycle schemes, etc.

Leaders lead by example with no / limited ' out of hours' work and connectivity.

Work \ Life
Pressure & Resilience

A key factor to your personal wellbeing is accepting that life naturally has up's and down's, and it is how we 'ride' those waves that is important, whilst most importantly remembering that for every down there will be another up in time.

The more we can smooth out those ups and down like a gentle roller coaster (or a sine wave) the better. Forcing or encouraging huge step changes (like a square wave) in our lives (or even in our thinking) should be avoided as this is rather like climbing a sheer cliff face, when you could also just climb the gradual hill.

The next section is part our process around appropriate work pressure and achieving wellbeing more generally in our lives. It offers further clarification of pressure (good) versus stress (bad) and the many things we can all do to help avoid that.

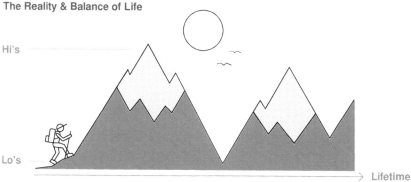

The Reality & Balance of Life

Richard Carlson \

Be grateful in your highs and graceful in your lows.

\ Psychotherapist

What is Stress?

The Health and Safety
Executives (HSE)
definition of stress is:

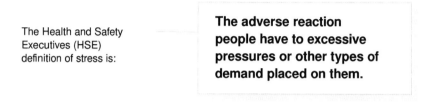

**The adverse reaction
people have to excessive
pressures or other types of
demand placed on them.**

This makes an important distinction between pressure,
which can be a positive if managed correctly, and stress
that can be bad for your health.

Another definition considers
your perception:

**Stress occurs when your
perceived pressure exceeds
your perceived ability to cope.**

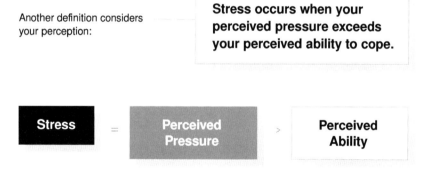

Therefore, we take the approach that **any form of stress
could be bad for you**, however being under pressure
often improves performance and can be a good thing,
it is only when it is excessive that it leads to stress that
could be bad for your health.

The graph below shows how pressure can 'stimulate' the body and enhance performance in the workplace, hence the term 'I perform better under pressure' (from Harvard physiologist, Walter Cannons research). If this condition is allowed to go unchecked however the person's health will degenerate as demonstrated below.

The Effects of Pressure on Performance

Performance

Optimum

Reduced Efficiency

Reduced Alertness

Effective

Overload

Creative

Difficulty Concentrating

Decisive

Indecisive

Alert

Irritable

Stimulated

Anxious

Confused

Under-involvement

Fatigue

Boredom

Exhaustion

Frustration

Burn-out

Rust-out

Pressure

The symptoms of stress are believed to come from our primitive 'fight, flight or freeze' response to perceived dangers.

It's believed that we have kept much our primitive hormonal and chemical defence mechanisms throughout the centuries which enabled the prehistoric person to either fight the perceived danger, run away or freeze and be eaten, thus the phrase 'fight or flight'.

In reality the lifestyle and culture that we live in today does not allow us to react physically to the problems that we face. We are not for example able to punch our boss when they are acting aggressively as such action is quite rightly not acceptable. Similarly, we are not able to use the 'flight' response either. You are not for example likely to flee from a stressful meeting, as again the behaviour would be seen as abnormal and the resulting consequences may be even more stressful.

It is believed that it is this denial of our primitive reactions that causes the strains on our body and leads to stress related disease and sickness, as the adrenaline and other chemicals that runs through our body and prepares us for our basic responses has no outlet.

I like to consider pressure using an **'Elastic band'** analogy – it can expand under **tension / pressure**, but still returns to its **normal shape** after a reasonable period – if however it is **under tension too long,** or expands beyond its **limits** then it will go past its **breaking point** and then there is no return. This would be comparable to someone effectively burning out in the above graph.

Anglepoise Approach to
Stress Prevention & Management

Our approach is firstly understanding how important eliminating stress is and aiming to achieve the right level of pressure for anyone at any given time (taking into account life's up and downs as mentioned above).

So, via risk assessment, we have many approaches covered in this book and elsewhere, that tackle this area from many different angles.

We also make sure we have a culture where everyone knows they can raise concerns, and their concerns will be treated seriously, sympathetically and with urgency.

Workplace Hazards that could
Cause Work Related Stress

Workplace hazards that could cause work related stress stem from many possible sources. The HSE provide guidance that suggests there are seven major causes of stressors or hazards that should be considered when conducting a stress risk assessment for the workplace.

Culture

of the company and how it deals
with work related stress (for example,
is there a long hour's culture?).

Demands

such as workload and exposure
to physical hazards (for example,
complexity and volume of work,
shift work, exposure to hazardous
substances and environments, etc.).

Control

how much say the person has
in the way they do their work
(for example are people involved
in deciding what work they do,
and when and how they do it?).

Relationships

includes all work relationships
(for example covering issues such
as bullying and harassment).

Support

from colleagues and line management.

Role

whether people understand their
role in the company, and whether
the company helps ensures that
they do not have conflicting roles.

Factors

unique to the individual allowing for
individual differences (for example
factors covered by the any form of
discrimination – age, gender, race,
disability, culture, religion, etc.).

Change

how organisational change is managed
and communicated in the organisation
(for example peoples understanding
why change is necessary).

Training

for everyone to be able to undertake
the core functions of their job.

What are the Personal Effects of Stress?

This table highlights the effects increasing work pressure can have on the body, both positive and negative, including some of the symptoms of stress. It could also be used as a guide to self-awareness of when you are feeling reasonable pressure, or when you are actually under stress.

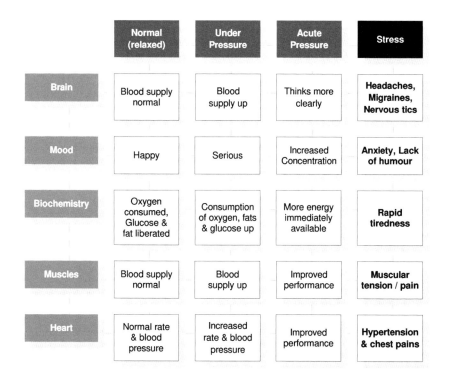

	Normal (relaxed)	Under Pressure	Acute Pressure	Stress
Brain	Blood supply normal	Blood supply up	Thinks more clearly	**Headaches, Migraines, Nervous tics**
Mood	Happy	Serious	Increased Concentration	**Anxiety, Lack of humour**
Biochemistry	Oxygen consumed, Glucose & fat liberated	Consumption of oxygen, fats & glucose up	More energy immediately available	**Rapid tiredness**
Muscles	Blood supply normal	Blood supply up	Improved performance	**Muscular tension / pain**
Heart	Normal rate & blood pressure	Increased rate & blood pressure	Improved performance	**Hypertension & chest pains**

	Normal (relaxed)	Under Pressure	Acute Pressure	Stress
Lungs	Normal respiration	Increased respiration	Improved performance	**Cough & asthma**
Saliva	Normal	Reduced	Reduced	**Dry mouth, lump in throat**
Stomach	Normal blood supply & acid secretion	Reduced blood supply, increased acid	Reduced blood supply & digestion	**Ulcers (heartburn & indigestion)**
Bowels	Normal blood supply & bowel activity	Reduced blood supply, increased bowel activity	Reduced blood supply & digestion	**Abdominal pain & diarrhoea**
Bladder	Normal	Frequent urination	Frequent urination (increased nerves)	**Frequent urination, Prostate symptoms**
Sex Organs	(M) Normal	(M) Impotence (decreased blood supply)	(M) Impotence (decreased blood supply)	**(M) Impotence**
	(F) Normal periods	(F) Irregular periods	(F) Irregular periods	**(F) Menstrual disorders**
Skin	Healthy	Dry skin (decreased blood supply)	Dry skin (decreased blood supply)	**Dryness & rashes**

What are the High-level Outcomes of Stress?

The figure to the right shows the relationship between the causal hazards identified above, the symptoms of stress for the individual and organisation, and the negative outcome (clearly highlighting why stress must be eliminated).

What can you do to Tackle Stress?

If you ever feel that your work is exposing you to excessive pressure and you may be developing symptoms of stress then we would strongly encourage you to do the following:

Firstly, talk to someone about it – raise any issues or concerns with your line manager, any senior manager, Health & Safety Officer or GP.

Try some of suggestions below in the section Individual Techniques for Coping with Pressure.

Accept opportunities for professional counselling and support when recommended.

Model of Work Stress
(Palmer, Cooper and Thomas 2004)

POTENTIAL HAZARDS	SYMPTOMS OF STRESS	NEGATIVE OUTCOMES
Culture	**Individual Symptoms**	**Individual Outcomes**
Demands	Raised blood pressure	Heart disease
Control	Sleep & gastro issues	RSI
	Increased alcohol / caffeine / nicotine	Anxiety & depression
Role	Increased irritability & negative emotions	Burnout
	Back pains; tension	
	Palpitations; headaches	
Change	**Organisational Symptoms**	**Organisational Outcomes**
Relationships	Increase sick absence	Increased overheads
	Long hours culture	Reduced profits
Support, Training & Unique Factors	Increased staff turnover	Increased accidents
	Reduced performance	Increased litigation
	Reduced morale / loyalty	
	Increased hostility	

Individual Techniques
for Coping with Pressure

Find out the things that work for you and help you relax and make them a **regular habit and routine**.

When busy or feeling under pressure, the things that help you relax are the first to be ignored. For example, you may feel too busy to exercise but these are the things that help you to relax enabling you to manage your time in a more productive way, both at home and at work.

Finally remember, if you are feeling that pressure in your work or life is becoming overwhelming – **talk to someone about it**, the road to recovery starts from there.

Here are some initial suggestions that may help
(see following page):

Relax

Make an agreement with a friend to be open about stress, and spot changes in each other – a stress buddy! Often you won't notice the changes in yourself when they will.

Take some exercise such as gym, swimming, walking, racket sports, yoga – whatever works for you.

Make some quiet time for yourself. Listen to some music or have a relaxing bath.

Take **Mindfulness** training and adopt those techniques into your daily life to be more in the moment.

Don't work too long at one task – take a break.

Laughter often relieves stress and tension – play games, watch TV, socialise, etc.

Think Constructively & with Perspective

We all make mistakes and we don't always get it right first time. Congratulate yourself when plans are going well, and just learn from your mistakes – that's how we improve.

Ask for help when you feel it is necessary – it is not a sign of weakness, just how we develop, and by talking with other colleagues, they may well be feeling the pressure too.

Plan

Make the time to plan – plan your work, your day, your week – use Outlook.

Write down all the things you are worried about they are often not quite as bad as previously thought, this also makes it easier to form a plan of action.

Set realistic achievable goals for yourself and reward yourself when you have achieved them.

Put tasks in order of priority. Plan your life – but be prepared to make changes.

Consider What You Eat

A balanced diet and regular meals will help you to cope with stress.

Drink plenty of water / fluids (but not too much alcohol or caffeine!).

Exercise

Exercise regularly – there is a proven feel good factor and strong evidence that this is a major help in dealing with stress. If exercise is undertaken it can take three to four weeks before it is enjoyed so persevere. So, find what works for you and you enjoy and just do it.

Leadership

87 – 132

If your actions inspire others to dream more, learn more, do more and become more, then you are a leader.

Stephen Covey \

Leadership is
a choice not
a position.

\ Businessman

We Are All Leaders
Playing to Our Strengths

 ## Leadership

Leadership is so much more than a job title, in fact, it's really nothing to do with your job title as most 'senior' positions in many businesses are 'management' roles, whereas anyone could be a leader in any role, leading by example, to inspire, encourage and get the best out of everyone around them.

(As mentioned in Chap – 2 and Chap – 5) at Anglepoise we use the Excellence Model (courtesy EFQM) to help guide our business planning, prioritisation and execution. The following section is taken from the excellence model and sets out what excellence in leadership could look like, and where appropriate points to specific sections in this book that explains our approach to it.

Leading with Vision, Inspiration & Integrity
(Excellence Model, EFQM)

Excellent organisations have leaders who shape the future and make it happen, acting as role models for its values and ethics.

In practice, we find that excellent organisations have leaders who embody the following:

Culture of Involvement

Inspire people and create a culture of involvement, ownership, empowerment, improvement and accountability through their actions, behaviours and experience.
(see Chap – 2)

Clear Direction

Set and communicate a clear direction and strategic focus; they unite their people to share and achieve the organisation's Mission, Vision and strategic goals. (see Chap – 2)

Innovation

Promote a **culture** which supports the generation of **new ideas** and new ways of thinking to encourage **innovation** and organisational **development**. (see Chap – 5)

Role Models

Champion the organisation's **values** and are **role models** for integrity, social responsibility and ethical behaviour, both internally and externally.

Flexibility

Are **flexible**; they demonstrate their ability to make sound, timely **decisions**, based on available information, previous experience and knowledge, with consideration of their potential **impact**.

Integrity

Are **transparent** and **accountable** to their stakeholders and society at large for their **performance** and ensure their people act **ethically**, **responsibly** and with **integrity**.
(see Chap – 1, and Chap – 3)

Here are two statements that all Leaders and
Managers at Anglepoise should aspire to:

Engaging Leaders are at the **heart** of an
organisations culture – they **facilitate** and
empower rather than control or restrict their
team; they treat their team with **appreciation**
and **respect** and show commitment to
developing, increasing and **rewarding** the
capabilities of those they lead.

Engaging Leaders offer **clarity** for what
is **expected** from individual team members,
which involves some **stretch**, and much
appreciation and **feedback / coaching**
and training. They also **treat** their people
as **individuals**, with **fairness** and **respect**
and with a concern for their **wellbeing**.
Lastly, leaders have a very important role
in ensuring that work is designed **efficiently**
and **effectively**.

Our Leadership &
Management Behaviours

The behaviours and qualities of Leadership & Management are very different things, but can, and should complement each other very well in different roles.

There are many definitions available for what is a Leader or a Manager (and many are contradictory), so the definitions below aim to help clarify this.

Leader   [lee-der] *noun*

A **Leader** is someone who **leads by example**, so that others are **inspired** and **motivated** to **follow** them. They **influence** a group of people towards the **achievement** of a plan or goal.

Manager   [man-i-jer] *noun*

A **Manager** is responsible for **planning** and **directing** the work of a group of individuals, **monitoring** their work, and taking **corrective action** when necessary. They are also often responsible for **budget** and **expenditure** and are normally the decision makers.

The following table further sets out the behaviours that are expected from all Leaders and Managers at Anglepoise:

All Leaders / Managers should	What this means
Let your team know what you expect from them	Be clear about the **outcomes** you want, and what the **boundaries** are (e.g. time, budget, customer requirements, etc.). Check that you have **communicated** with them **effectively**, and they can reflect back their understanding to your satisfaction.
Share information with your team	We all need to know what is going on and why. There has to be a very good reason to keep information confidential.
Allow team members to do it their own way (set clear boundaries and outcomes)	If we do it our own way, we can **play to our strengths**. If we do it our manager's way, we cannot play to our strengths. So, **manage on outcomes** (with **clear boundaries** such as complying with company policies and procedures), not the way we get there. Also seek feedback for understanding from your team to ensure everyone is aligned.
Let your team do more (delegate)	We must not believe that only we can do some things. Take a risk and **delegate more** (taking into account their experience, skills and abilities).
Trust all colleagues and believe the best of them	Trust does not need to be earned by our colleagues. **We trust each other to do the right thing** (again taking into account their experience, skills and abilities).
Celebrate mistakes... and learn from them	We learn and grow by making mistakes and learning from them. **No one makes a mistake on purpose** so when they happen let's get to the underlying cause and improve the system.

$\rightarrow$

All Leaders / Managers should	**What this means**
Get your team the things they need to do a good job	Ensure your team have access to the **tools, material** and **support** they need to deliver the outcomes you want.
Let your teamwork things out for themselves	**We learn by trying things.** If we have all the answers our colleagues will never have a chance to learn.
Listen and enquire – be able to receive feedback	**Listen** to what your team is saying and ask questions to help you **genuinely understand.** You must be able to receive feedback (good or bad), and **focus on the issue,** not the person providing it – i.e. is the feedback valid; can it be cross checked; what will you do about it.
Provide constructive feedback to your team, whatever the circumstances	You must be able to **give feedback** (good or bad) to your team and individuals, and not shy away from the tough issues that may confront you.
Set up your team to succeed, exploit strengths	Give your team the opportunities to **play to their strengths** and **do what they do best every day.**
Help your team to feel good about themselves	Happy colleagues deliver better service. As leaders it's a key part of our role to give regular **recognition and praise.**
Take full responsibility for your life at work	**The only person we can control is our self.** If we want things to change, we must do something about it our self. If we wait for someone else to fix our problems, we may have a long wait.
Encourage your team to discover how they want to develop and help and support them	Anglepoise will **continually improve** if we all individually improve. Leaders must help their team to develop in their chosen way.

As leaders we must constantly reflect on what we do, and then learn and develop better ways of using our own strengths to live out these principals.

Leading by Example
(acting as a Role Model)

The most common saying around good leadership is to always 'Lead by example' or 'Act as a Role Model' – of course this works both ways in that if you're setting a poor example with your behaviours and actions then you can't expect others to follow and exhibit different, better, behaviours.

Therefore as we strive to lead with the behaviours described above, it's worth returning to the importance of having no **'SAY / DO gap'** (as mentioned in Chap – 3), we should always strive for no SAY / DO gap as this is the best way to lead by example.

So stop talking about stuff, actually do it, plan it in and get it done, how much time do we spend talking about the things that we should just get on with – **say what you're going to do, why you're going to do it, and get it done**.

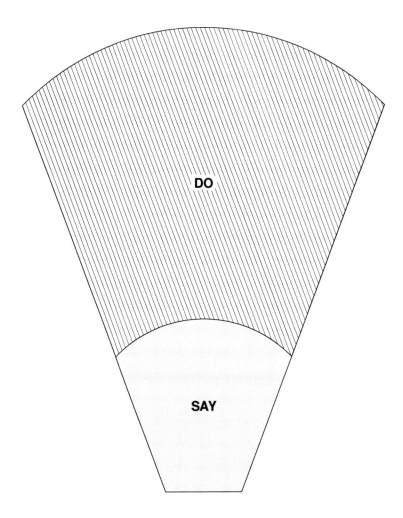

Teamwork \
Built on Trust

You can't be a leader without a team around you, and we
fundamentally believe that all team work starts with **trust**,
and this trust does not need to be earned, but is taken as
a given – that everyone wants to do a good job, and so
believe the best in them and trust them.

There is also strong research on consistent high performing
teams that of the 3 keys traits or behaviours for success –
Trust, Respect and Like – that the 'Like' element is really
not that important compared to Trust and Respect for long
term sustainable high performing teams. In fact, >80% of the
sustainable success of the team is due to them all trusting
and respecting one another, whereas liking each other has
a much smaller part to play.

Leaders who focus disproportionately (perhaps manipulatively)
on their colleagues 'liking' them will only get short term success,
if there isn't the strong core of team trust and respect.

Traits of High Performing Teams

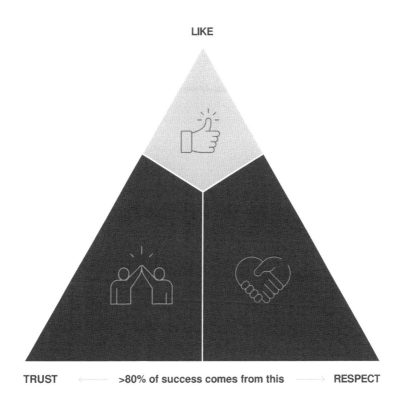

Trust is the Foundation
for People Engagement

Another area we believe is crucial for People Engagement (see Chap – 2) is that **trust must also be the foundation for engagement**, which then leads to outstanding **results**.

In the 'Engagement House' below you can see the foundation of trust creating authentic conversations, leading to team engagement, then personal accountability, all accumulating in consistent, outstanding results (the following two sections are adapted from work by Warwick Cavell).

Teamwork & People Engagement
is built on a Foundation of Trust

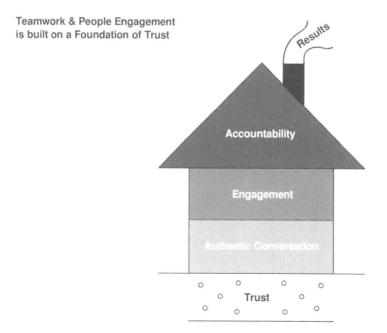

Terminology

What do we mean by each term?

Trust

You will look after my **best interests** when I'm **vulnerable** (works all ways: Individuals ⟷ Colleagues ⟷ Anglepoise).

Accountability

Everyone takes **intellectual** and **emotional ownership** of their tasks.

Authentic Conversation

Meaningful, **open**, **honest** involvement and **two-way** communications.

Results

Consistent and **outstanding** performance and results.

Engagement

Creating an **environment** where everyone is **motivated** to want to connect with their work and really **care** about doing a **great** job.

Creating **opportunities** for everyone to **connect** with their colleagues, managers and wider organisation. It is a concept that places **flexibility**, **change** and **continuous improvement** at the heart of what it means to work at Anglepoise.

Trust and the Behaviours we look for at Anglepoise?

OPENNESS
"I give & ask for feedback freely"

- Being non secretive
- Volunteering information
- Keeping people informed (no surprises)
- Sharing your feelings (good and bad)
- Asking for feedback
- Adequate access to each other
- I can ask for help when in need

RELIABILITY
"I'll do what I say I'll do"

- Keeping promises (I'll get my task done)
- Being dependable (I won't let the team down)
- Maintaining confidences
- Being punctual
- Following through on detail
- Accepting responsibility
- Competence

CONGRUENCE
"What I say is what I mean"

- Being direct with people
- Saying no when you mean no
- Clarifying expectations of others
- Practicing what you preach
- Facing up to conflict
- Honesty

ACCEPTANCE
"Who you are is OK with me"

- Non-judgemental of people
- Non-critical of people's differences
- Not talking down to people (jargon)
- Mutual respect
- Permission to make mistakes
- Listening

Trust, Self-worth and Motivation

The diagram below also underlines the importance of trust (in Anglepoise and each other), including how engaged you are. We strive for everyone to be a genuine **Volunteer** (real people engagement leads to this).

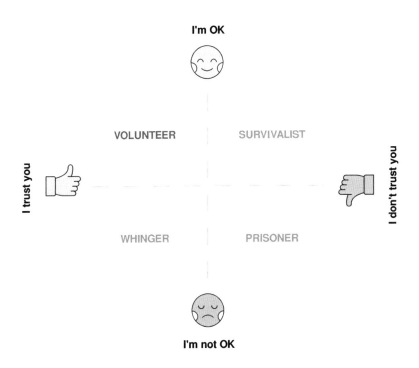

Trust, Self-worth & Motivation

Prisoners

At the darkest end of the workplace lives the Prisoner. This person has low self-worth and also hates the company, their leaders and workmates. They act as though they are in a jail, saying, "I have to get out of here", and "I can't wait to escape on Friday".

Survivalists

Survivalists are those people who have high levels of self-worth, but for whatever reason do not have a high regard for their colleagues, leaders or the company. They will follow all published rules, appear as Volunteers, but at the moment of Truth will fall away and look after their own interests before everything else.

Whingers

Whingers are people with low levels of self-worth, created from whatever reasons – personal, family, peers or environment. They have high levels of trust in those around them and thus become dependent on those people. In the case of the leader or manager, this often emerges as complaints, demands, cries for help and criticism of others to the boss.

Volunteers

Volunteers have high levels of trust and self-worth – they will give everything for their job, their colleagues and the business. They both engender leadership and energise people to follow them – this is where we all want to be.

Team Building & Excellent Team Working

The following section is from our **Team Building training**
and helps us all to understand the important of our teams
and why and how they will always outperform the individual.

What is a Team?

In current society 'teams' are considered familiar and
commonplace, but many years ago workplaces were mainly
based on vertical hierarchies with rigid job descriptions that
defined the individual's contribution to the whole.

These days organisations are generally much 'flatter' and
there is an expectation for more flexible roles. Also, life is far
more democratic now and the involvement and consultation
of everyone to achieve a common goal is much more normal,
and in most cases essential.

Teams could be considered as:

Groups of people with a **common goal** who
use the **unique** strengths of **each member**
and the **combined** strengths of the group to
achieve that goal.

Teams within Anglepoise or any business could include: Sales and Marketing, Accounts, Warehouse, Customer Support, Design, Leadership, Board of Directors, the whole company, etc. So, in all businesses, large and small, there are many teams, some fixed, some more transient, but all crucial to the success of everyone else.

Characteristics of High Performing Teams

The following are typical characteristics and behaviours of high performing and effective teams:

Trust, value and respect other members of the team, leading to openness and constructive feedback (no fear of reprisal).

Committed to excellence and delighting the customer.

Persistent in pursuit of goals – action oriented and creatively flexible in getting there.

Prepared to confront people and situations obstructing progress.

Tenacious and inventive in removing obstacles.

High expectations of themselves and others.

Inspired with a strong sense of purpose whilst understanding strategy and 'the bigger picture'.

Actively build networks of people who can help them and welcomes advice from others.

Visible and accessible.

Communicate strongly what they stand for and within the team, encourage paraphrasing to avoid miscommunication.

All team members are considered equal, irrespective of position in organisation.

Ensures every team member is involved and understands reasons for decisions.

Operation of the team is informal, 'people friendly' and they have fun and enjoy themselves.

Driven by success and thrive on it.

Responds quickly and positively to problems and opportunities.

Expect leader to fight for support and resource.

Prepared to take legitimate risk.

Constantly looking for ways to improve.

As you've read through the recommendations above, consider what behaviours you most exhibit and try and create and build upon these characteristics within the teams that you work in.

Groups Vs Teams

There are some fundamental differences between a 'group'
of people and a 'team' and therefore why a team will always
be more successful. The table below summarises some of
these different qualities:

Groups	Teams
No leader	Must have a leader
No overriding vision	Vision and goals provided by the leader or by consensus
Subgroups formed randomly	Focus on working together as a single group
No communication procedure	Communication procedure in place (doesn't need to be written down, just understood by all members)
No support for each other's activities	Support for each other's activities
No group identity	Self-esteem formed through group identity
Individual contributions not encouraged or relevant	Individual contributions welcomed

A group does not automatically become a team. It takes work and effort from each individual member to ensure that team characteristics are created within any collections of people that you work with. One of the most important competencies to achieve this is good communication.

Try to look out for when you are in a group rather than a team, and where appropriate take positive action.

Model of Team Development

So how do groups become teams and then how do teams develop? The model of team development below (by Bruce Tuckman) found that during their operational life teams may go through 4 distinct stages, these are:

1   **Forming**

2   **Storming**

3   **Norming**

4   **Performing**

1 Forming

This is the settling in period. There is a certain amount of confusion and anxiety while people begin to relate to other team members. The behaviour at this stage is typically polite and superficial.

Actions required to move to the next stage are:

\ Clarify the team's **purpose** and **goals**

\ Establish **roles** and **responsibilities** of the individual team members

\ Define the process for **planning actions**

\ Define **procedures**

2 Storming

In this stage people are beginning to 'flex their muscles' in terms of their roles. Individuals may be beginning to compete with one another. Some people will try to dominate, and cliques may develop. There are various bids for power and influence, which may take the form of outright confrontation. There may be covert support for those wishing to take control on the part of the less vocal members.

Actions required to move to the next stage are:

\ Clarify how the **team** is going to **work**

\ Define the ground rules for **listening** and **managing conflict**

\ Encourage **input** from everyone

3	**Norming**

In this stage people start to take responsibility and perform their team roles. The team acts as a team and not a group of self-interested individuals. Levels of trust increase, and the team begins to work together. Contributions from the various individuals are recognised.

Actions required to move to the next stage are:

\ Define stretched **performance targets**

\ Encourage the team to **challenge** its way of working

4	**Performing**

This is the stage where team members are cooperating fully in order to achieve goals. The team is working at peak performance.

Actions required to move to the next stage are:

\ Continue to **monitor goals** and **challenge** any **complacency**

5	**Mourning**

There is also considered to be a fifth stage of 'Mourning', where the team has been disbanded or significantly changed (where it may then return back to 'Forming').

Team Roles & Personal Strengths

A significant outcome of the research carried out by
Dr Meredith Belbin was that there are 8 unique roles that
would prove beneficial in a **well-balanced** and consistently
successful team.

Most of us will have **strengths** in a variety of these roles
but are also likely to have **one** or **two dominant behaviours**
that will significantly influence your role within the team.

By completing a brief team role questionnaire, you can
determine which characteristics you have strengths in and
therefore where in a team you will most enjoy being part of,
and also excel in project and task execution.

Remember there is no **good or bad** with these roles,
only that a team needs **balance** to be **successful**.

Also, even if you haven't completed the questionnaire,
as you read through the following key different team role
types think about which one you're most like and where
you can therefore contribute most and be more successful
within your teams (see www.belbin.com).

CO-ORDINATOR

PLANT

A **co-ordinator** is a likely candidate for the **chairperson** of a team, since they have a talent for stepping back to see the big picture. Co-ordinators are **confident, stable** and **mature** and because they recognise abilities in others, they are very good at delegating tasks to the right person.

The co-ordinator clarifies decisions, helping everyone else focus on their tasks. Co-ordinators are sometimes perceived to be manipulative and will tend to delegate all work, leaving nothing but the delegating for them to do.

Plants are **creative, unorthodox** and **generators** of **ideas**. If an **innovative** solution to a problem is needed, a Plant is a good person to ask. A good Plant will be bright and free-thinking. Plants can tend to ignore incidentals and refrain from getting bogged down in detail. The Plant bears a strong resemblance to the popular caricature of the absent-minded professor / inventor, and often has a hard time communicating ideas to others.

Multiple Plants in a team can lead to misunderstandings, as many ideas are generated without sufficient discernment or the impetus to follow the ideas through to action. Plants can also create problems with the timing of their ideas. The fact that the team has decided on a valid way forward and is now in the implementation stage will not stop the Plant from coming up with new solutions and disrupting the implementation process.

INVESTIGATOR

SHAPER

The **Resource Investigator** gives a team a rush of **enthusiasm** at the start of the project by vigorously **pursuing contacts** and **opportunities**. They are focused outside the team and have a finger firmly on the pulse of the outside world.

Where a Plant creates new ideas, a Resource Investigator will quite happily appropriate them from other companies or people.

A good Resource Investigator is a maker of possibilities and an excellent networker, but has a tendency to lose momentum towards the end of a project and to forget small details.

The **Shaper** is a **task-focused** individual who **pursues objectives** with **vigour** and who is driven by **tremendous energy** and the need to **get things done** – for the Shaper, achieving is the name of the game. The Shaper provides the necessary drive to ensure that the team is kept moving and does not lose focus or momentum.

Shapers are people who challenge the team to improve. They are dynamic and usually extroverted people who enjoy stimulating others, questioning norms, and finding the best approaches for solving problems. The Shaper is the one who shakes things up to make sure that all possibilities are considered and that the team does not become complacent.

Shapers could risk becoming aggressive and bad humoured in their attempts to get things done. Shapers often see obstacles as exciting challenges, and they tend to have the courage to push on when others feel like quitting.

EVALUATOR

TEAMWORKER

Monitor Evaluators are **fair** and **logical** observers and judges of what is going on in the team. Since they are good at detaching themselves from bias, they are often the ones to see all available options with the greatest **clarity** and **impartiality**.

They take a broad view when problem-solving, and by moving slowly and **analytically**, will almost always come to the right decision. However, they can become very critical, damping enthusiasm for anything without logical grounds, and they have a hard time inspiring themselves or others to be passionate about their work.

A **Teamworker** is the oil between the cogs that keeps the machine that is the team running smoothly. They are **good listeners** and **diplomats**, talented at smoothing over conflicts and helping parties understand one another without becoming confrontational.

Since the role can be a low-profile one, the beneficial effect of a Team worker can go unnoticed and unappreciated until they are absent, when the team begins to argue, and small but important things cease to happen. Because of an unwillingness to take sides, a Team worker may not be able to take decisive action when it's needed.

IMPLEMENTER

COMPLETER

The **Implementer** takes their colleagues' suggestions and ideas and **turns** them into **positive action**. They are **efficient** and **selfdisciplined** and can always be relied on to deliver on time.

They are motivated by their loyalty to the team or company, which means that they will often take on jobs everyone else avoids or dislikes. However, they may be seen as closed-minded and inflexible since they will often have difficulty deviating from their own well-thought-out plans, especially if such a deviation compromises efficiency or threatens well-established practices.

The **Completer Finisher** is a **perfectionist** and will often go the extra mile to make sure everything is **"just right"** and the things they deliver can be trusted to have been double-checked and then checked again.

The Completer Finisher has a strong inward sense of the need for **accuracy** and sets his or her own high standards rather than working on the encouragement of others. They may frustrate their teammates by worrying excessively about minor details and by refusing to delegate tasks that they do not trust anyone else to perform.

An effective team does not need to include every role, but from research over many years it has been found that a successful performing team must at least include one person from each of the left and right sides in the diagram below. It is also important to recognise that in the execution of a task or project, different roles become important at different stages in the process.

Team Based Project \
Task Execution
using Belbin Roles

COMPLETER

4

FINISH

EVALUATOR

IMPLEMENTER

3

TEAMWORKER

SHAPER

1

CO-ORDINATOR

PLANT

INVESTIGATOR

2

Personal Development

Another crucial part of leadership is developing yourself and others in your team. Always mutually looking for ways to turn your talents in to your strengths (see start of Chap – 3), and therefore do more of what you instinctively love doing and finding the contented state of flow and being 'in the zone'.

The section below is part of our Personal Development Review Process which is conducted annually but then followed up with monthly 1 to 1's to ensure that the agreed development and actions are still valid and good progress is being made.

Personal Development Reviews
Skills for Success

In order for a Personal Development Review (PDR) process to be successful at least six skills are needed equally by both people. These skills are not only critical to the success of the PDR, they are also critical to your personal career success in any position.

1   **Time Management**

2   **Assertiveness**

3   **Listening**

4   **Goal Setting**

5   **Coaching**

6   **Tracking Results**

1	**Time Management**

For the development review to be successful everyone needs to complete their part of the process on a timely basis. Your Line Manager will schedule your review, and your **responsiveness** to their request for a meeting date, and subsequent preparatory actions shows **respect** for them and this process.

Many time management experts suggest that the best way to tell what is important to someone is to look at their calendar. If our colleagues are our most important asset, setting aside time for feedback and development must be one of our top priorities (see Chap – 5 for further suggestions and advice on improving your time management and efficiency).

2	**Assertiveness**

Empowerment requires assertiveness but many of us have not learned how to act assertively. In our society there are a lot more passive or aggressive role models than there are assertive ones.

Passive people are often victims, they let others control and influence them. On the other hand, aggressive people are often perceived as abusive or manipulative, they run all over others. There is a third option – assertiveness.

Assertive people know how to express their needs or feelings in a way that doesn't upset or offend others. They do so by using 'I' statements. For example, if your Manager cancels your meeting, rather than passively withdrawing or aggressively criticizing, you can respond with an "I" message – "I feel disappointed (frustrated, etc.) because we have to cancel our meeting. When are you available to reschedule?" It may seem easier to feel victimized than it is to learn to be assertive, however, the pay-off for learning this skill is huge. It can enable you to make things happen in a positive way in all aspects of your life.

$\rightarrow$

3	Listening

A good development review discussion requires two-way communication. Both you and your Manager should be **equally** involved in speaking and listening. Both parties need to demonstrate their **active** listening skills.

Active listening as opposed to passive listening, means taking the time to find out if you truly understand what the other person said. Words are tricky, they don't always have universal meanings. What one person hears is not necessarily what the other person meant. The only way to prevent misunderstanding is to practice active listening by taking the time to **check for understanding**.

Paraphrasing or summarizing what you think you heard and asking for more information / explanation are good active listening tools. For example, if your Manager says: "I'm really surprised by what you described as your biggest accomplishment", try not to jump to conclusions and immediately start defending your choice or become angry. Instead, ask for clarification. You might say: "What surprises you?" You may find that your Manager was surprised because they had totally forgotten about that major success. Never jump to conclusions about another's comments without taking the time to clarify.

Each party should approach the development meeting with a willingness to **seek first to understand, before being understood**.

2 ears

1 mouth

Remember, you have 2 ears and 1 mouth
Use them **proportionally!**

Goal Setting

The heart of the development review is goal setting for continuous improvement – for you and for Anglepoise. In order to contribute effectively you need clear direction. This direction comes through the goal setting process. A good goal generally has SMART characteristics:

It begins with an action verb, then be...

SPECIFIC   **M**EASURABLE   **A**CHIEVABLE   **R**EALISTIC   **T**IME-BOUND

Below are some example goals that meet these criteria. Typically, most goals will be in the next 6 to 12 months, although it may depend where you are in your career. It's possible that no goals are appropriate, and this is acceptable, but generally development is more likely when specific goals are set and therefore effort should be put into achieving this.

Complete **project X** by **30th November**

Create **3 relevant newsletter** items by **next review**

Improve customer **feedback scores to X** average by **30th June**

Improve communications skills by attending a **1 day training course** and reviewing skills learned with Manager prior to **next review**

Deploy new sales campaign for **X market** by **31st March**

Complete **First Aid training** by **28th February**

$\rightarrow$

Using action verbs to write a goal helps you to focus on what you want to accomplish. Some useful **action verbs** to consider are:

Goals should be specific so that there is no ambiguity in how they could be read and understood. A good goal is always **measurable**. In other words, two or more people would wall have some criteria by which they could agree whether or not it has been met.

It is also important that the goal is **achievable** (is it possible for you to make this happen?) and **realistic** (you might say that 100% of time should be spent calling customers – possibly achievable but not very realistic given other activities).

It is up to you and your Manager to determine what is **realistically** achievable within a specific time period given the resources available and the other expectations already in place. Sometimes it may be necessary to carry over goals from one year to the next due to the shifting priorities of the team or company.

The final characteristic of a valid goal is that it has clear **time expectations**. The due dates for most goals will be the date of the next development review session. If a goal needs to be completed prior to the next development session, the target date should be clearly indicated and then reviewed at a monthly 1–1.

5	Coaching

None of us ever outgrow our need for feedback and support. Without assistance from others, we tend to stay stuck in old beliefs and behaviours even though things around us are changing very quickly. In the traditional workplace, the Manager was the one who gave feedback and coaching. In team-based work environments, we **all** need to learn to act as coaches. Good coaches:

- **Encourage** their team members to use more of their **strengths**

- **Encourage** their team members to do **their best**

- **Recognize** and **celebrate** team members' **accomplishments**

- Provide **timely** and specific **feedback** to team members when requested

- Share **knowledge** and **experience** with the team

What could happen to your engagement and your colleagues or team's productivity, if **everyone** at Anglepoise took regular time to coach their fellow team members?

6	Tracking Results

Both you and your Manager should track progress toward your agreed goals. There are many ways to achieve this but using a simple form, like a Success Log, can achieve this purpose.

Ongoing development tracking enables both you and your Manager to have more objective development discussions. Without this information two laws of human behaviour tend to influence development discussions:

$\rightarrow$

The law of recency is the tendency to remember (and discuss) only recent development rather than review the entire development period.

The law of negativity is the tendency to remember mistakes more clearly than successes.

Keeping a real time success log can neutralize these human barriers to objective development reviews and maximise the overall benefit gained.

Communication & 1 to 1's

This final section on leadership briefly covers the importance of regular and appropriate communication and how we suggest monthly 1 to 1's can be conducted (but this is flexible to suit the needs of the individual).

The 1 to 1 Process

Timing & Preparation

1 to 1 meetings should normally be held once every 4 to 6 weeks, and typically last between 30 minutes to an hour. It is recommended to book the meetings in advance using Outlook, perhaps at the end of each meeting.

As with all meetings suitable preparation is essential to maximise the success of the meeting. Therefore, plan time beforehand to ensure all relevant information is prepared and reviewed (e.g. development actions; Balanced Scorecard information; other actions lists; strengths profile; etc.).

Recommended Discussion Points

The 1 to 1 process is designed to be informal and flexible to meet the needs of the individual and the management style of the Line Manager. The following are recommended discussion points at each 1 to 1 meeting:

Start by discussing how they are feeling and any personal work highlights since last meeting, and if appropriate link back to their personal strengths.

Discuss other work activities since the last 1 to 1, especially identifying any particular achievements or challenges. This provides an opportunity to identify any skill gaps together with any training requirements.

$\rightarrow$

Review any training and development activities since last
1 to 1 and check that skills and knowledge are being applied.

Check if any training and development is planned and if
appropriate arrange a pre-training briefing before the event.

Review and discuss any actions from the previous 1 to 1 or annual
goals and targets from the Personal Development Review process
– aligning to the current Balanced Scorecard results where possible.

Discuss planned work activities over the next six weeks or so with
a view to highlighting any imbalance in workload, together with any
potential problems or coaching requirements.

Encourage discussion of any areas of concern that they may have,
these may be skills, personal, organisational, etc.

Feedback should be given to the individual on performance since the
last 1 to 1, in particular acknowledging achievements. Any areas for
improvement should be discussed with a view to establishing a SMART
development plan. Part of the line manager's preparation for the meeting
will be to gather relevant information and review the previous PDR.

Encourage discussion of any feedback on Compass meetings,
the management team and company direction etc.

Any relevant actions coming out of the 1 to 1 are recorded
along with the responsibility and due date for those actions
(this could be via a spreadsheet or update to the PDR).

Discuss any company documents that have been issued
recently ensuring that they have been read and understood.

Specific Discussion Points

There may be specific discussion points that should be raised at the 1 to 1 meeting as informed by the Leadership Team. These topics may be updated quarterly, and the response should be captured and summarised to the appropriate Manager.

Motivation

The 1 to 1 process is a good opportunity to provide individual motivation. Here are some practical points to consider:

Make everyone feel valued by:

- Genuinely sharing an interest in whatever they hold important

- Creating an atmosphere of approval and co-operation

- Ensuring everyone understands the importance of their contribution to the team's and companies' objectives (via the Balanced Scorecard where possible)

- Regularly reviewing everyone's work and achievements

Provide scope for development by:

- Setting appropriate SMART targets

- Providing on and off the job training and coaching

- Arranging any necessary internal and external contacts

$\rightarrow$

\ Using colleagues to train others in specialist skills they may have

\ Restructuring or grouping tasks to use everyone's strengths to the fullest

Recognise achievements by:

\ Praising and communicating individual succes

\ Reporting regularly on the team's progress

\ Regular meetings to monitor and counsel on an individual's progress
towards targets

\ Explaining overall company results and achievements

Provide challenge by:

\ Setting and communicating the team's objectives

\ Providing scope for individuals to take greater responsibility

\ Encouraging ideas and continuous improvement, and where possible
by allowing individual responsibility for implementing them

Excellence

133 – 168

Excellence is not a gift, but a skill that takes practice.

We do not act rightly because we are excellent, in fact we achieve excellence by acting rightly.

Aristotle \

We are what we repeatedly do. Excellence then, is not an act, but a habit.

\ Greek Philosopher

Continuous Improvement
Along the Journey

 Excellence

There are many definitions of excellence, but fundamentally for us it's all about always looking for better ways to do things. Whether that's looking at 'marginal gains', '1% improvements' or 'incremental innovation', or using techniques such as why / why analysis, process mapping or root cause analysis, etc. – they all lead to continually questioning everything we do and making, often small, gradual improvements across all that we do.

I've mentioned previously that we embrace the Excellence Model as our key framework for pursuing excellence across the business and also in the short, medium and long term, the section below will cover our approach in more detail and also why we started using it in the first place.

We also talk about our '**Journey to Excellence**' as in reality we will always be on this journey, striving to improve and basically makes things easier and better for all concerned. We will never reach the destination of 'excellence' as those goal posts will always, quite rightly, keeping moving, stretching us further, but providing priorities and focus along the way.

Pursuing excellence (or continuous improvement) is part of a company's culture, something that becomes an element of your DNA and therefore part of everyone's habits and routines on a daily, weekly and monthly basis.

Excellence is also about 'doing' things, looking for and making those changes and useful improvements, hence why I've included a section below on 'Making the most of our time – getting things done'.

When we're considering 'excellence' it is also crucial that we remember our '**Balance in Life**' – the imperative importance of work / life balance, family, friends, personal development, health, diet, exercise, and so on, and therefore excellence must take into account all the key parts of that equation, also measuring and monitoring that balance is being achieved (a key part of our focus on 'Legacy').

Excellence is also covered in many other areas of this book, particularly at the start. For excellence to be just 'what we do' (or aspire to), it must form part of our fundamental values (personally and as a business), and therefore also part of all of our approaches. Take recruitment for instance, we always aim to recruit on **attitude**, **aptitude** and **personal values**, and then train for skills, as it's the foundation of personal excellence that will drive the continuous improvement culture of the company.

Excellence therefore starts with purpose and why and ends with our legacy (or at least the ongoing journey to leave the world in a better place).

The Excellence Model
& Us

I think it may be useful at a high level to understand why we chose the Excellence Model, how we broadly use it and what we've learned so far, so that we have some perspective of how it all fits together and how it fundamentally helps us.

But before we get to that... what is the Excellence Model?

There is a significant amount of information available regarding the history of the model and its extensive use across a wide variety of businesses, charities and academic institutions, etc. and so I won't go into that detail here, but I think it's worth highlighting that the model / framework on page 141 is based upon the 'Fundamental Principles' (on the right), all of which link into our values and vision.

Excellence Definition
from EQFM 2013:

Excellent organisations achieve and sustain outstanding levels of performance that meet or exceed the expectations of all their stakeholders.

Fundamental Concepts of Excellence
© EQFM 2013

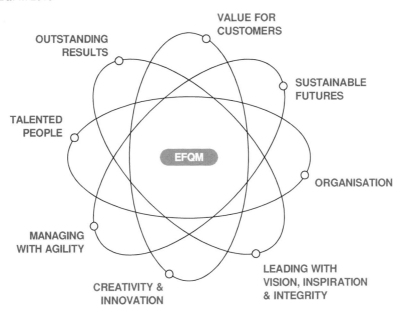

The definition rightly focusses on sustainable levels of outstanding performance, thus you must be able to prove **long term confidence** (cause and effect), and improvements across all areas of the model and therefore your business, and that you are fundamentally delivering your strategy and that meets or exceeds what all of your key stakeholders need (stakeholders are basically all the key people and parties connected to the business – employees, suppliers, shareholders, banks, society etc.).

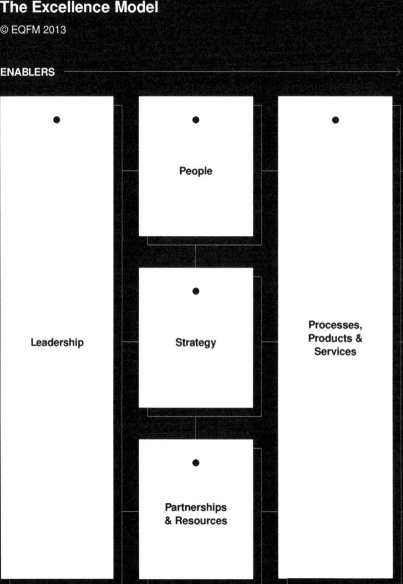

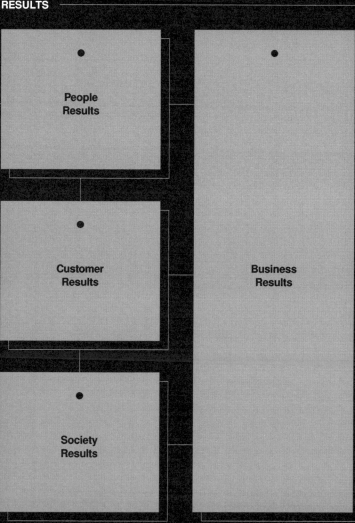

The model itself sets out the framework of what excellence looks like in each of the nine key areas – five '**Enablers**', effectively what makes everything happen; and four '**Results**', all the things we should measure to ensure we're delivering our strategy in a balanced and sustainable way.

Each of the areas above then have much more detail behind them, typically four or five other key focus areas with many examples of what excellence can be, whilst still being flexible to suit the needs of **any** organisation.

I've mentioned the RADAR process (from EFQM) in Chap – 2. RADAR is actually used as the key measurement tool when conducting an excellence assessment (across each of the nine areas of the model), but we've embraced it more widely as a great approach to take that reminds us that we should always start with the end in mind and understand the fundamental why and purpose for all that we do.

Using the process (to the right) we start with step 1 before any other action is taken to ensure the purpose and desired result is actually worth doing and meets the overall plan (or strategy). Only then do we move to planning and developing the approach that will be taken to achieve the desired results, before moving to actually deploying that approach, and then finally, and very importantly, assessing and refining the approach and deployment to see how we can improve in the future (for this we also use a Project Debrief process when appropriate) – all part of the journey to excellence.

Projects \ Actions
RADAR Always start with the end in mind

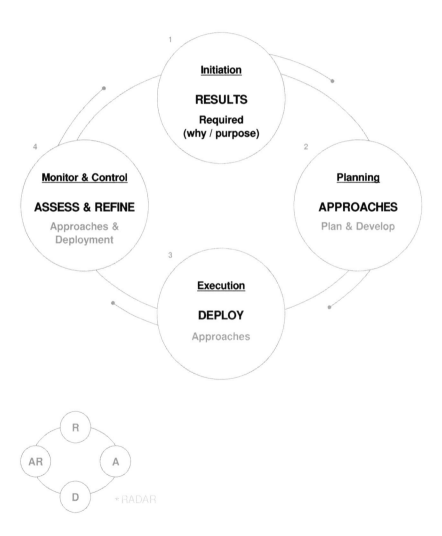

Anglepoise Excellence Journey so far

Some years ago, I was looking for a companywide strategic planning and measurement structure that would pull together many of the other things that we were doing into a cohesive whole, so that we had a long-term framework to help drive our strategy, prioritisation, focus and excellence.

Here's a brief summary of the key activities and processes we had in place prior to using the Excellence Model, all of which we continue to use but now within its overarching framework:

\ Created our **Vision, Purpose, Values, Mission**, etc.

\ Annual **strategic process** (where appropriate using PESTLE, SWOT, Porters)

\ **'Great Place to Work'** framework and action plan – based on 'Best Companies', Gallup and 'Investors in People' approaches

\ **ISO approaches** to quality and other internal processes

\ Annual **People Engagement** surveys and actions based on Gallup Q12

Once we had decided to embrace the Excellence Model and use it across the business these are some of the key steps, we took to successfully embed it:

\ Getting started and obtaining 'buy in' – sold the **Excellence strategy and action plan** to the Board / SLT

\ Joined the BQF (EFQM representatives in the UK)

\ Attended excellence model assessor **training**, became **qualified**, and joined their model user group

$\rightarrow$

\ Visited other **model users** and **winners** – Ricoh; St Monica Trust; Winchester University – many, if not all model users I've met are very happy to share learnings and best practice

\ Shared our **Excellence plan** company wide

\ Used **appropriate language** (cut the jargon), and repetition!

\ Completed our first **internal excellence assessment** (after training and qualification)

\ Set up '**Excellence Teams**' – leader and 'volunteers' to action assessment outcomes via **excellence projects**

One of the great benefits of using the model and annual assessment is how it helps to prioritise and focus excellence activities to suit your business and strategy. At Anglepoise here are some examples of our initial and ongoing activities on the journey to excellence:

\ Established our '**Balanced Scorecard**' and departmental key metrics (see Chap – 2) – used for assessing monthly / quarterly / annual targets against our Mission and providing everyone with clarity

\ Ongoing '**Excellence Projects**' – initially 50+ including some of the following:

   \ Develop / expand '**Delight the Customer**' strategy, including **Net Promoter surveys**, etc.

   \ Develop / implement **long term IT plan** (infrastructure; ERP; Sharepoint; Intra / Extranet; CRM; etc.)

   \ Define and broaden our **Charity** and **Community Support** activities (Society) and determine plan for **Society perception measures** / performance indicators, then deploy

   \ Create process for identifying **Partnerships** and **Collaborations**

   \ Develop companywide **Process ownership**, and continuous improvement of all processes

\ Continue annual **People Engagement** survey (based on Gallup Q12)

\ Conduct annual internal **excellence assessments** to measure progress, determine key action priorities and set new targets

---

We're now well into our excellence journey
but what are our key learnings so far?

\ It **takes longer** than you think, generally we were too optimistic on delivery of excellence projects

\ Always use **appropriate language** – consider what words / phrases people will really understand, and how that will 'stick' to become part of just what we do and say, a new part to our culture

\ Always be conscious of the **SAY / DO gap** – mentioned a few times in this book and critical to the success of companywide change – if you say you're going to do something – do it

\ Repetition, repetition, repetition – it takes time for things to sink in and become part of our culture

\ Make everything **habit** and **routine** – it just becomes what we do

\ Plagiarise with pride – make the best use of the excellence community, all of the other model users are very open to sharing best practice – learn, adapt, make it work and improve

\ Always '**Ask Why?**'

That wraps up our focus on the Excellence model and our journey so far, the following section is about understanding how we make the most of our time to actually get things done along with focussing on continuous improvement.

Making the Most of Time \
Getting Things Done

This section is mostly around 'Time Management' which can sound pretty boring as a topic, but you need to remember that the more that we get out of our time the more content we will be in our lives.

Time in a day or week is finite, we cannot create more time, just make better use of what we have. If you choose to do something you may be sacrificing the time for something else, so **choose wisely**, and make the most of it.

It may seem a little selfish but when considering your time it's worth thinking about 'What's in it for me?', 'How can I make my life easier or more enjoyable?', 'How can I do more of what I want to do?' – making the most of our time will help achieve that.

Before we get into the recommendations around time management, we should always remind ourselves to start with the end in mind, ask yourself – 'Does this even need doing?' – I like to think that this is the first rule of **time management** – if something doesn't need doing then time management is irrelevant, just don't do it and choose to do something else that's actually needed and useful – again, as always, **ask why**.

It's also worth looking out for overlaps, or touch points between activities and people, i.e. if two people are duplicating certain parts of their work. Consider a 'Sales Manager' and 'Customer Support' team, ideally they should have clear boundaries so that there's only a very small amount of overlap and hopefully no duplication or wasted effort, even down to too many people reading the same email when in reality only person needed to.

Imagine the hands below are individual people or roles, ideally we want the lightest overlap, or touch point possible:

Ideally Minimal Overlap Between Roles:

Heavy Overlap = Avoid

Light Overlap = Ideal

Time Management Best Practice

To improve your time management, it is important to remember that you need to find what will actually work for you. It's unlikely that you will just be able to copy exactly what someone else does who is very efficient with their time and so over the following pages think about what is most likely to work for you – adapt it, try it out and then adapt again to get the most out of your time.

The following section covers best practice tools & techniques that can assist and improve your time management, but it will only work if you choose to embrace it and actively make it happen.

Do You Think You Need Time Management?

Consider the following statements – what category do you fall into at the moment, and where do you ideally want to be?

1

I choose what I do and when I do it.

2

Much of my time is used reacting to the demands of others and the system, but I still have some free time that I can use in the way I wish.

Of course, ideally, we probably all want to be statement 1, but in practical terms it's more realistic to aim for between 1 and 2.

3

All of my time is taken up reacting to the demands of others and the system. I hardly ever have any free time that is truly under my control.

4

There is never enough time to even satisfy the demands of others and the system. I always feel like I'm behind and struggling to catch up.

It's also interesting to consider the same statements for your work and personal lives – if there is a difference, ask yourself why, and also keep in mind your personal life 'time management' over the following sections.

How Important is Time, and Why?

Do you feel that you have less time now than five or ten years ago? – for your family, friends, hobbies, work, etc. – if so why? In the modern world we all seem to have more options, more information, more choice – but it is your choice – should we prioritise – be more selective in what we choose to do?

To gain some perspective on the importance of time it's worth remembering that if you can turn just 1 unproductive hour a working day into a productive one, you effectively add / gain 7 working weeks to your year!

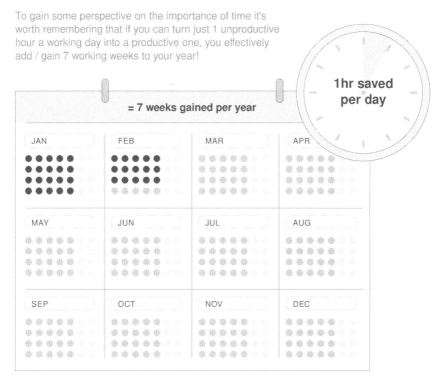

= 7 weeks gained per year

1hr saved per day

JAN	FEB	MAR	APR
MAY	JUN	JUL	AUG
SEP	OCT	NOV	DEC

(1 x 5 x 52 = 260 hours; 260 / 37.5 = 7 weeks)
Imagine what else you could be doing with that time.

What is the 'Value' of Your Time?

What value are you adding to yourself and the business?
Clearly there is a cost for anyone in a business and they need
to contribute at least that value otherwise there would be
no benefit. Consider also the 'cost' of meetings where many
people attend – is it necessary, who really needs to be there,
is it unnecessarily long?

Does Anyone 'Value' Their Time Outside of Work?

What jobs do you pay others to do for you (that you could
do yourself, like washing your car)? If you're choosing to pay
others to do jobs for you then you probably feel your 'value'
is worth more than that cost (although this is probably a
subconscious decision, not maths based).

**Improving time management generally in your
life can allow more time for family, hobbies, etc.**

What is Time Management?

It's more about management, than time. Writing everything down in a diary or task list can provide clarity of what you think you need to do but is it actually **worth** doing.

Another thought to consider – remember the last time you went on holiday – did you achieve a lot more than normal in the few days before going? Tying up loose ends, tidying things up, making sure things were taken care of before you left. What techniques did you employ? Could you repeat them? If you were going away tomorrow, how differently would you work through today, would you be a better time manager?

Multi-tasking \
To be Avoided?

There was a period of time where multi-tasking was seen as an ideal way of productively working, but research has shown that it should be avoided where possible.

This research shows that the brain needs a **'warm-up'** period of time when preparing for a new activity. Once this is done your mind is 'primed' to work productively. But even a 30 second distraction can be enough to **'derail'** this, and the whole process then needs to be repeated. This can lead to as much as **20% to 40%** of your time being **wasted** (equal to 1.5 to 3 hours per day).

So, it's best to allocate time to **specific tasks** and then **focus** on **completing them**. Tell people what you are doing to minimise interruption, perhaps consider working from home, or in a quieter space in the office for those particular tasks.

Another benefit of not multi-tasking is that it reduces the likelihood of over-runs. For instance, if there are 3 tasks to be completed, and they are effectively done in parallel, then there is a 100% chance one of them will not be completed by the deadline. Whereas if each task is completed in one go then there is only a 33% chance that one task will be late.

Consider the diagrams below:
The Over-run Risk of Multi-tasking

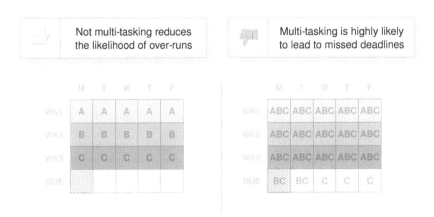

| | Not multi-tasking reduces the likelihood of over-runs | | Multi-tasking is highly likely to lead to missed deadlines |

	M	T	W	T	F
WK1	A	A	A	A	A
WK2	B	B	B	B	B
WK3	C	C	C	C	C
DUE					

	M	T	W	T	F
WK1	ABC	ABC	ABC	ABC	ABC
WK2	ABC	ABC	ABC	ABC	ABC
WK3	ABC	ABC	ABC	ABC	ABC
DUE	BC	BC	C	C	C

Avoiding multi-tasking shouldn't be confused with not having lots of different things to do. It means you should prioritise and focus on getting each one done in one go, rather than doing bits of each activity and not actually finishing them off.

Also, there are some instances where multi-tasking may be beneficial, e.g. when answering the phone, you might be printing out some documents, etc.

Remember:
Break all Large Tasks into Bite-sized Chunks

Focus & Energy

Before we look at time management best practice specifically we should also consider where we need to be as individuals to actually make a difference in the jobs that we do, and how personal change in our behaviours can be achieved (again the following model is based on significant research).

What is Personal Focus & Energy?

Focus   Concentrated attention (set clear goals and see them through to completion)

Energy   Passion, enthusiasm, motivation, and personal commitment

What happens as the level of focus and energy changes with us as individuals? Consider the diagram (on the following page) which also shows the typical % of people in an average business:

Excellence

Disengaged

Can see the right course of action but don't do anything about it due to low motivation. They retreat to comfort activities and avoid risks.

Purposeful

Can achieve critical long-term goals, by identifying importance and seeing them through. They will feel that they are vital to the business.

Procrastinator

Seems like too much to do; can't get started on anything (rabbit in headlights).

Distracted

All action, but not on important issues – Shoot first, aim later. Firefighting. Overloaded. Things don't get finished. Always looking for new things (more fires to light?).

Hi

Lo

FOCUS

Lo   ENERGY   Hi

Key:
Typical % of people in an average business

| 40% | 30% | 20% | 10% |

The **purposeful** decide what must be achieved and then **manage** the **environment** around them. The others look to **outside forces** (bosses, peers, salaries, job description, etc.) to decide what is feasible (or not), and then let those factors **control** and **constrain** them.

The purposeful realise that they are **masters of their own destiny** and use their focus and energy to determine and achieve their goals.

Using the suggestions in this book consider how you can become 'purposeful', plan how you will get there, and then develop habits and routines to stay there.

What 'Wastes' Most of Your Time?

Taking into account some of the approaches mentioned so far, it's worth making a list of all the things (work and home) that you consider a 'waste' or unproductive use of your time, e.g:

Unnecessary or over-long **meetings**	Being **interrupted** (breaking your 'flow')	Doing something **manually** that could be automated

Writing or reviewing unnecessary **reports** (interesting, but so what…)	Reading **emails** that don't concern you (plague of email politics & cc'ing everyone!)

So, being completely honest with yourself, take a few moments to draw up this list and if appropriate assign the amount of time 'wasted' per week, either by hour or % of your time (and bear in mind that 1 hour saved a day = 7 weeks gained in a year).

Then assess what you can stop doing, prioritise the rest, and use some of the following suggested techniques to be more effective and make best use of your time.

The Balance
Important Vs Urgent

All of life's tasks fall into the grid below, consider what key tasks you do and where they currently fall:

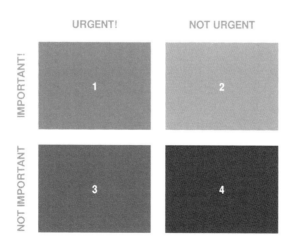

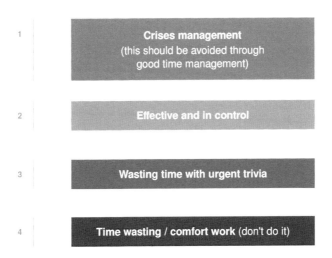

Clearly, we all ideally want to be in zone 2 – **effective** and in **control**, completing **important** tasks but not when they're **urgent** (and then likely to be rushed and mistakes are made).

Therefore, with all of the tasks that you do at work or in your life, consider their **importance** and **urgency**, and then take appropriate action.

Time Management
Tools & Techniques

Remember time management is more about management, than time.

Common tools that are used for making the most of your time – Outlook (by far the most effective), To Do lists, Task lists, MS Project, Excel (as a planner), etc. – consider each of these tools and how well they work for you. Task or to do lists for instance – do you always consistently complete all the tasks and on time? If not, why not? Is it visual enough for you, and flexible to meet the daily demands or your role?

The most important thing is that you find what **works for you** personally and consistently delivers on time results, and then live by it (daily habits and routines) to make the tool most effective.

It's also worth understanding if you generally think in terms of hours, days or weeks – if you generally look at an overall week only, but then often you're late on a short daily task, then break the tasks into smaller chunks (say down to the hour), focus on that task and get it done.

Efficiency Suggestions

Plan Weekly

Plan on a **weekly** basis (then review daily), it provides better balance, context and flexibility. Perhaps every Friday afternoon so that you know what you're doing the following week and can relax over the weekend.

(tip: set a 30-minute recurring event in Outlook every Friday pm to plan in this weekly activity)

Then for each of your typical weekly activities you should consider if they are **Important** and / or **Urgent** (i.e. which area do they fall into in the table in the above section), and then take appropriate action.

Consider how long you think you should be spending on them and assign a time (or percentage).

Review

Review this regularly, ideally **daily**, and be **flexible**. Don't let the plan become a millstone. Update your plans and times and learn from your experience.

Discuss

Discuss these activities with your line manager, task manager, or colleagues. Sharing this information acts as a good **benchmark** and helps to educate others how long certain tasks can take and why.

Do It

Do it – be **ruthless** with the implementation of your plans, be **competitive**.

You may want to also consider measuring fairly accurately what you actually do every day, over a few weeks. You will probably be surprised by how many hours are spent dealing with unnecessary email, or administration tasks.

Question everything that you do and ask, 'Is this necessary?'

Tips to Manage Your Email

How many unread emails are in your inbox? – imagine that was paperwork on your desk, would you still behave the same way?

Checking Emails

Only check your email 4 or 5 times a day (say every 2 hours), it will radically **reduce** the amount of **distractions** and keep you focussed on completing the task in hand. Remember, truly urgent messages are more likely to be delivered in person or over the phone.

Email Control

Never handle mail or email more than **once**, either **deal with it, file it, delegate it, or delete it**. Where possible ensure that 'spurious' or 'irrelevant' documents don't reach you at all.

Communication Method

For **teams, agree a communication method** that allows a simpler identification of messages and required action. (e.g. start your email topic with the customer name)

Notifications

Only check emails when you want to – so **turn off notifications and pop ups** – they are just a distraction and time waster.

Screen Messages

If you don't recognise the sender or topic – then **mark it as junk** (block sender), or just delete it.

Unsubscribe

Unsubscribe from annoying or unnecessary newsgroups. Even if they are occasionally interesting (but not **essential**). The distraction and additional time wasted is unlikely to outweigh any benefit.

Normal Post

If you are regularly receiving brochures or newsletters that aren't particularly useful then get removed from the mailing list.

Where Can You Start?

Pick a cut-off date (say 6 or 12 months) and archive all messages prior to that. If they are not required after for instance, 6 months, then delete it.

Set up your new regime and stick to it. Put reminders in the calendar, diary, task list, etc. (whatever **works for you**).

Remember, if you don't do anything, then nothing will change or improve.

Other Useful Efficiency Tips

Peak Performance

Know your 'peak' performance – work out what times of the day you work at your best and set aside activities for then that require the greatest concentration.

Delegate

Where you can, and where appropriate (pick tasks for people's **strengths**).

Trust Instincts

Keep asking yourself the following question – "What is the highest and **best use of my time right now**?" and **trust your instincts**.

Organise

Organise your desk – whatever works for you – prioritise – trays, folders, maintain an 'essential' workspace. With **paperwork – either deal with it, file it, delegate it, or bin it**.

Remember – as with all **continuous improvement** and **personal development** it cannot be effective unless you **choose** to do **something positive** about it – set yourself some actions and do them **today**.

Other Useful Efficiency Tips

Minimise Interruptions

Work from home (where practical and always considering your customers and colleagues).

Inform people what you are doing, and that you are working to a deadline.

Say to people 'Can I **get back to you** by....', rather than interrupting what you are doing.

Use the right **body language** – don't give time away.

Follow email tips – **turn off notifications and pop ups!**

Extra Work

If you think that taking on **extra work** could jeopardise the customer relationship / project etc. then once you've thought it through, justified it and discussed with you line manager – say no.

Disciplined & Flexible

Be **disciplined** and yet **flexible**. Reflect on what you have learned and make changes.

Interesting & Non-essential

When you receive emails or documents that are **Interesting but not Essential** – put these to one side, collect them to read once a week. If you then find you didn't have time, delete them.

Our Legacy

169 – 176

We do not inherit the Earth from our ancestors; we borrow it from our children.

James Kerr \

Be a good ancestor, plant trees you'll never see.

\ Writer

Doing the Right Thing Now
For the Future

 Legacy

What is a **Legacy** – quite simply it's what you leave behind once you move on… but it's worth remembering that it could be good, bad or indifferent, so it is your choices and actions in your lifetime that will define that legacy.

For us our legacy is leaving the world (in that we have some influence) in a better place, or better than where we found it.

Our legacy is always based on '**doing the right thing now for the future**' and that is in all things that we do as a business, from designing and producing lights that people can truly value, **love** and be **proud** of, to reaching out and giving something back to the **societies** that we work with and helping them where we can, from Universities and mentoring for small businesses, to volunteering and raising money for local charities.

We also always look to truly work in **partnership** with all people and companies within our growing network, for the **long term greater good** of us all. This is fundamentally based on our shared **values** and **beliefs**, one of which is that we're not here to make money, that is just a means to an end, but we're here to always be striving to achieve our **vision** and **purpose**, improving all that we do – be that our culture, people, customers and products, so that, in our small way, we're helping support the future and next generation.

When considering the environment and our influence on the world, whilst we do focus on recycling, reusing and reducing our impact where possible, our fundamental approach and legacy is offering a **lifetime guarantee** on our products, truly a **'lamp for life'** – fighting the modern throwaway thinking of society and engendering a lifelong relationship with our lights.

> **Another of our key aspirations is from our focus on a 'Great Place to Work' and particularly around personal wellbeing and mental health. We hope that part of our legacy will be to have raised awareness and helped, for our part, to ending mental health discrimination (both professionally in the workplace and personally in our lives).**

Our pledge and commitment to **'Time to Change'** is so important to us that I want to briefly revisit it here. At its most simple this is about enabling everyone to talk about their mental health like they would their physical health, without any judgement or concern, so that we can all help find the right support and make changes to suit our personal needs.

So, if there is only one thing that you take away from this book then I would like it to be the understanding of the critical importance of mental health and what we can all do to take steps to remove the stigma and discrimination that affects one in four of us every year.

Overall whilst we have many successful approaches and actions around time to change and creating a great place to work that are described in detail in previous chapters, we hope from a legacy perspective that we've created a culture that truly provides **balance** and **flexibility** in life, providing everyone with the opportunity to personally develop, pursue wellbeing and choose what's right for them, whilst enjoying the journey and continually progressing towards achieving our overall purpose and goals.

These are our legacy aspirations at Anglepoise… but what will be **your legacy**, what **choices** will you make, and how will **you** make it happen?

ANGLEPOISE®

Published by Anglepoise
Written by John Purnell
Copyright © John Purnell, 2020

Design by Jazzy Olive

Cover Artwork & Illustration Assistance
Anastassia Spirkina (founder of doubles_creative),
Leonie Summer, and Natalia Nowakowska

www.anglepoise.com